TRACK DAY DRIVER'S GUIDE

TRACK DAY
Driver's Guide

**How to prepare your car and
yourself for the thrills of
high-speed circuit driving**

ART MARKUS

MRP

First published in 2002 by
MRP Publishing Ltd, PO Box 1318, Croydon, Surrey, CR9 5YP

A catalogue record for this book is available from the British Library.

ISBN 1 899870 59 8

Typesetting and origination by Jack Andrews Design, Westerham, Kent
Printed and bound in Great Britain by MPG Books Ltd, Bodmin, Cornwall

CONTENTS

Nowadays, you don't have to be one of the gods of motorsport to enjoy access to the world's greatest motor racing circuits, like Spa-Francorchamps, in Belgium, with its downhill entry into the testing Eau Rouge bend. In 2001 readers of CCC Magazine competed for five free VIP track passes for a two-day event held there in conjunction with Demon Tweeks, Wheeltorque and the Gold Track Driving Club. Inset: Jo Siffert and Pedro Rodriguez putting on a virtuoso display in their Porsche 917s to win the Spa 1000 Kilometres race in 1970.

INTRODUCTION

The motor car, despite its many critics, is a marvellous invention which has brought joy to millions in the form of mobility and personal freedom. For the vast majority of motorists the car is merely a means of transport, but for a few of us it is more . . . much more. Some of us have a *passion* for cars and for driving. If you are reading this it is a virtual certainty that you are one of us: a motor enthusiast . . . a car nut . . . a petrolhead. All we need to attain our own personal *nirvana* is a fast car, a full tank of fuel and a clear road ahead.

Sadly, though, in much of the developed world the joy of the open road is no more. The car may promise mobility and personal freedom undreamed of by our ancestors, but as ever more people are able to buy into the dream, so it turns into a nightmare of congestion, pollution, regulation and oppression. Too many cars, and too few roads, means increasing competition for precious road space. Traffic jams and road works, sleeping policemen and other traffic calming schemes (a misnomer if ever there was one!), speed cameras and radar traps; all are symptoms of overcrowded roads and conspire to make road travel a chore rather than a pleasure . . . purgatory for those who really *love* cars.

At the same time, a lot of the fun has also gone out of motorsport. Because so much motor racing – Formula One especially – is now beamed into millions of homes live via satellite there is an unstated

desire to make it absolutely safe so as to avoid any repetition of the death of Ayrton Senna in 1994, a tragedy made immeasurably worse as it was watched live by millions on prime-time television. However, this continued endeavour to make motor racing safe at any cost is misguided and ultimately futile. Regrettably, some great circuits have been spoiled as a result, or have fallen into disuse as their operators were unable or unwilling to meet the latest safety standards. Motor racing worships at the altar of safety, and sadly this permeates through even to amateur club racing, which finds itself ever more regulated and stifled by bureaucracy.

There is an answer though. If you want to enjoy the freedom of the open road, unfettered by all the usual restrictions of road travel or organized motorsports competition, you should attend one of the many track days taking place at circuits all over Britain, and indeed Europe, predominantly during the summer months.

Track days give you the opportunity to test your car on some of Europe's most famous motor racing circuits, like Spa-Francorchamps, Silverstone, Monza, Brands Hatch and, the granddaddy of them all, the mighty Nürburgring Nordschleife. For many years, those legendary venues were the exclusive preserve of the elite of motorsports and remained largely inaccessible to even leading amateur competitors, but now, thanks to the boom in popularity of track days, they are accessible to the ordinary road car driver. By attending a track day you can take on the challenge of the world's greatest circuits, follow in the wheel tracks of your motorsports heroes, become a better driver, and enjoy driving your car to its maximum potential.

This book tells you all you need to know to get the best out of your car . . . and yourself. Whether you are a track day virgin or veteran, and whether you drive a bog standard road car or one fully prepared to competition specification, you will find there is much to be learned within these pages. You will learn how to prepare your car – and yourself – for your first track day; how to optimize your seating position; how to choose and use safety equipment; what you can do to improve the performance of your car; track day etiquette; and much more besides. In the chapters on driving you can learn about vehicle dynamics; what happens when you are cornering at speed; how to get the most out of your tyres; how to recognize the limit; how to find the fastest – and the safest – line; how to avoid mistakes . . . and what to do when you do err; how to drive a wet track; how to handle kerbs and other hazards; and much else.

In order to make it more digestible, the book is divided into bite-sized chunks, or chapters. However, this may not always suit our purposes too well, especially when it comes to an analysis of motor vehicle dynamics. This is a complex subject, and the topics covered are interrelated to such an extent that it is difficult – and may even be counter-productive – to separate them. That is why, in order to 'pick up the thread' where necessary, there is some reiteration and why certain phrases appear in more than one place. I make no apology for that.

Also, because of the unavoidable complexity of the subject matter, the book will repay careful and perhaps repeated reading. Again, no apologies. Therefore I can't guarantee you a laugh a minute as you read it (it's not that kind of book!), but I *can* guarantee that you will have great fun putting into practice what you have learnt. I can also guarantee that when it comes to fast driving you *never* stop learning. You may find, therefore, that once you have one or more track days under your belt you will want to read certain sections or passages, or even the whole thing, once again. I hope so.

The very fact that you are reading this book suggests that we have much in common: a passion for fast cars, skilled driving . . . and speed. It represents the knowledge I have gained (sometimes painfully!) from a lifetime spent driving, testing and racing cars; writing about cars and driving technique, and reading what others have written; talking to other drivers about cars; thinking about them, and perhaps even dreaming about them at times! As such, writing it has been a labour of love. With luck, it will help you to get the maximum enjoyment and satisfaction from your track time. It may even help to make you a better driver. If so, I will be well satisfied. And if your passion for cars and driving gives you even a fraction of the fun I have enjoyed over the years, I will be more than just satisfied: I will be well pleased.

Keep it on the island . . . and have fun!

ART MARKUS

Ash Green, Surrey
January 2002

1

BIRTH OF THE TRACK DAY

Track days have become so popular in recent years that it is all too easy to take them for granted. Yet just a few years ago the idea of Joe Public being let loose on a race circuit was unthinkable. The only way to get onto a race circuit was to acquire a racing licence, at considerable expense; obtain, by some means or other, a suitable race car, inevitably at considerable expense; and enter a race at . . . you guessed it . . . considerable expense! And sometimes even that wasn't enough: some circuits were reserved more-or-less exclusively for major motorsports events, so it was a rare treat even for club racing drivers to use some of the great Grand Prix venues.

But today, ordinary motorists, in many cases driving ordinary everyday road cars, can enjoy access to race tracks all over the UK and Europe, including a number of the current and former Grand Prix circuits, and at moderate cost . . . most of the time at least. This has come about due to a combination of circumstances, most probably starting with the circuit owners seeking to maximize revenue.

Motor racing circuits, by their very nature, tend to occupy large tracts of land. However, racing takes place only at weekends, so in the past the land lay idle, and all the facilities and amenities provided for spectators, competitors, officials, etc, remained unused for much of the week. In the days when many UK circuits were little more than disused WW2 airfields, perhaps this did not matter terribly. However, over a considerable period of time, the circuits were required to provide more and better facilities, including well-equipped medical centres, administration buildings, pits buildings, grandstands, hospitality units, canteens, sales kiosks and so on . . . not to mention miles of Armco barriers and, more recently, acres of gravel traps. All of which demanded considerable expenditure.

Perhaps it was not realized immediately, but eventually it dawned on the circuit owners and operators that their circuits represented a substantial financial investment, and that using a circuit for theoretically no more than 52 weekends a year – and in practice much less of course – was a terrible waste of resources, so they were forced to look for new and imaginative ways to increase their revenues. Incredibly, the Indianapolis Motor Speedway, home of the famous Indy 500, was used for just that single event each year. Admittedly it was a *big* event, lasting most of the month of May and boasting the biggest one-day paid attendance of any sporting event in the world, yet even that couldn't last in the modern era, and nowadays the Indianapolis Motor Speedway hosts three major motorsports events a year: the Indianapolis 500 (IRL), the Brickyard 400 (NASCAR) and the US GP (F1).

Given that even the most popular circuits in Britain hosted no more than 30

Silverstone
The Home of British Motor Racing

Motor racing circuits like Silverstone, by their very nature, occupy a lot of land. As facilities improved over the years, and the investment in circuit infrastructure like control towers, grandstands, pit and paddock buildings, medical centres and so on became ever more substantial, circuit operators were forced to think of new and imaginative ways to increase revenue. Track days were just one result.

to 40 motorcycle or car race meetings per year, the obvious answer was to obtain more use from the facility during the week. Many of the circuits were opened for race car testing, and the majority hosted some form of race school. But the latter part of the 20th century brought much greater environmental awareness, and many circuits found that mid-week testing was severely constrained by ever stricter noise limits and local planning restrictions.

One solution was to open the circuit for normally silenced road cars. It also seems probable that the shrewder circuit operators realized they could earn more from hiring the circuit exclusively to one of the major motor manufacturers for a track day than they would from a motley collection of impecunious club racers out for a day's testing, and annoying the neighbours with their infernal racket! So manufacturer-based track days became popular in the 1980s and '90s, with BMW in the vanguard with its popular 'On Track' programme. Corporate 'action days' followed, often run by the race school based

Incredibly, the Indianapolis Motor Speedway was, for many years, used just once annually, for the famous 'Indy' 500. This is the start of the 1957 race.

at the circuit. From there it was just a short step to allowing the ordinary enthusiast motorist access to the circuit, and soon a host of track day organizers sprang into being to meet the growing demand for track time.

Undoubtedly this demand was fuelled, at least partially, by the considerable prosperity enjoyed by some in the latter years of the 20th century, when there were many enthusiasts with a lot of disposable income, a lot of leisure time and a hankering to spend both in pursuit of an adrenaline high!

Conversely, driving on the road, for any enthusiast with a high-performance car, was becoming a pain in the posterior. Too many cars and too few roads means that roads are always overcrowded, and congestion is a constant problem. Because the motorist makes such a huge contribution to its coffers, the government is unlikely to do anything that might reduce the number of vehicles on the road . . . quite the reverse in fact; so far as the Chancellor is concerned, the more the merrier! So this is a problem that can only get worse. Indeed, the government seems hell-bent on making the motorist pay, and

pay dearly, for his precious mobility. And with the police surrendering meekly in the fight against crime and declaring war on the motorist instead (let's face it, it's easier!), driving on the road is no longer any fun.

This confluence of events has given rise to the recent boom in track days, so there is now ample opportunity for anyone with a hankering to drive on a circuit to do so, even if they have no desire or intention to drive in competition. If you have always dreamed of driving on a circuit, now there really is no excuse not to.

The popularity of track days has been further fuelled by the fact that most modern cars – especially high-performance models – are reasonably able to cope with the demands of high-speed track use, even in standard form. Okay, this may be a dangerous generalization, for there are bound to be exceptions, as the circuit can expose weaknesses in a car – especially one with no sporting pretensions – that may never be apparent in normal road driving. However, these weaknesses are more likely to be in performance than in fundamental reliability or safety. Most modern cars will happily trundle around a race track without overheating, blowing up or breaking down, and will have at least reasonably decent roadholding and adequate brakes. Certainly this will hold true for the novice track day driver, who is unlikely – initially at least – to take his or her car to the outer edges of the performance envelope. Therefore you needn't assume that you need a specially prepared car, or a top-of-the-range sports model, in order to take to the track; your average well-maintained road car will be perfectly adequate.

It is possible, however, that it may not feel as quick as you thought. If you drive a reasonably modern high-performance car on the road you probably think it feels pretty rapid. Get it on a race track, though, and you may be in for quite a surprise. On the track the car is more likely to feel sluggish . . . unresponsive . . . with clumsy handling and dodgy brakes, because a race track has a way of making even the tautest road car feel out of its element. So a track day novice will do well to be prepared for

this; you may think you've been driving a real greyhound, and it turns out to be a poodle . . . or even a chihuahua!

There really is a huge difference between driving fast on the road and driving on a track. There are very few roads – in Britain at least – where you can drive for long at full throttle and sustained high rpm before you come across slower traffic, a built-up area or, increasingly (because they know where to site these things for maximum revenue!), speed cameras forcing you to slow down. After all, escaping all those constraints is one of the primary appeals of a track day. But however hard you might think you drive on the road, you can seldom if ever do so in the way you are able to on a circuit. This is where the car can really be stretched and when problems may be revealed which have never been apparent in normal everyday driving, such as a severe handling imbalance (understeer, usually), fading or pulling brakes or, most irritating of all, an engine misfire. These problems can be immensely

Modern high-performance cars like this BMW M3 are easily capable of taking the punishment dished out on a race circuit.

A major incentive to get your speed thrills on the circuit, not on the open road.

frustrating as they are intrinsically difficult to diagnose or cure at the track due to the lack of on-hand facilities, expertise, equipment, etc . . . and patience, usually.

Routine maintenance

The key to avoiding this sort of trouble is preparation; a few hours spent in routine maintenance can save a lot of time and frustration later. Remember you will ordinarily have paid a considerable sum of money for the track day, so it makes sense to maximize valuable track time, not waste it bleeding brakes, changing pads, or scratching your head trying to cure a misfire. If you are not a competent mechanic, you will need to engage a professional to prepare the car for you. If possible, you should take your car to a recognized marque expert, perhaps someone who is already engaged in motorsport preparation and understands the demands of track day driving. This is unlikely to be a main dealer! Ideally you need to find someone who will take a personal interest in you and your car, someone in whom you can come to trust.

Increased wear

When you do track days you will undoubtedly experience greatly accelerated wear on all consumables – tyres, brake pads, etc – which you must therefore monitor carefully. You should also expect greater oil consumption, so check your oil level regularly: before you start, obviously; after your first track session; during the lunchtime break; and – depending on the consumption levels you have experienced – mid-afternoon and/or before you drive home. You also need to budget for this greatly increased wear and tear. Ironically, a lot of people do track days because – they say – they can't afford to go motor racing, but because of the number of miles you can rack up on a track day you can 'hammer' the car far more than you would in the average 15-minute practice session and 10-lap club race. You may find you can clock up more miles in two or three track days than in a whole season of racing!

As a rough guide you can figure that each track day mile is worth about 10 road miles, perhaps more. Therefore you should anticipate more frequent rebuilds of major components, such as engine, gearbox and differential. Of course this will depend to some extent on how well you look after them and how hard you use them, but if you habitually thrash the engine to the redline at every opportunity, 'crash' your gearchanges, and spin the wheels whenever possible, you will inevitably pay the penalty in higher rebuild costs and possibly the occasional breakage. The single most important factor, though, is to make sure everything is thoroughly warmed up before you use the car hard.

Inevitably, winter is a good time for rebuilds, but it is also likely to be the busiest time for the specialists, which is a factor to bear in mind when planning maintenance. Incidentally, this accelerated wear rate is also a factor to bear in mind when scheduling routine servicing. For example, if you were to clock up 1000 miles on track days, you should then perform the equivalent of a 10,000-mile service. However, you must perform the routine safety checks – tyre condition and pressure, oil levels, brake pads, brake fluid, etc – before every event. If you prefer to leave this routine to the professionals, you should have them check the car over, if not before every event then certainly every other event. It should be obvious that checking the car more frequently than is strictly necessary is preferable to not checking it often enough, and over a period of time you will establish a pattern of wear that will dictate your maintenance schedule.

Well oiled

If you can believe the manufacturers' advertised claims, the latest synthetic-based oils are supposed to last much longer than conventional mineral-based oils, allowing service intervals between oil changes of 10,000 miles or even more. Sorry, but I don't buy it! If you only ever drove your car on the road, and you drove conservatively, seldom using full throttle and never using maximum revs, then the extended service intervals may be appropriate. Indeed, they may be fine for the average motorist (although even then I have my doubts) but they are *not* okay for the hard-driving enthusiast motorist.

Oil has a number of functions. Obviously, it lubricates. It also cools. Just as importantly, oil holds in suspension the contaminants created by combustion and

wear and tear on the engine: including carbon, acids, minute metal fragments and so on. These contaminants are what turn the oil black, and if you monitor your oil level regularly after an oil change you will know how quickly that happens. The oil effectively acts like a giant sponge, soaking up these contaminants, and transporting them to the filter or holding them where they can't do any harm. While synthetic oil may well retain the ability to cool and lubricate over extended service intervals, I wonder whether it is able to fulfil this latter function over an extended period. After all, the same contaminants are being generated regardless of the oil used: why should synthetic oil be able to absorb more of these contaminants than mineral oils, especially as the quantity contained in the sump remains unchanged? For that reason, and regardless of the manufacturer's claims, I recommend an oil change after 3000 miles of mixed road and track driving, and perhaps 1000 miles for pure track driving.

Log on

One of the problems you may find in scheduling servicing and routine maintenance is that keeping track of your track day mileage may be tricky, especially if you drive the car on the road regularly as well. The solution is to keep a log. When you are racing it is crucial to keep a log of all track miles, so you can monitor mileage between engine rebuilds for example. You can also monitor wear and tear including breakdowns and other failures, allowing you to 'life' components if necessary; record any modifications and improvements; keep on record the best set-up for each circuit; and generally analyse performance. It may not be essential for track days as you are not necessarily striving for the maximum performance at all times, but keeping a log is not a bad policy, for all of the same reasons. Although performance may not be as critical as when you are competing, reliability and safety most certainly are. And it is safety that I shall be discussing next.

2

SAFETY FAST

We motoring enthusiasts love to drive fast. But the reality is that driving fast is an inherently hazardous (I'm loathe to use the word dangerous!) activity, which is undoubtedly why we find it exciting . . . stimulating . . . exhilarating. Adrenaline is the drug, and we need to score! At the same time, when we go to a track day we don't want to hurt ourselves, so we need to take certain precautions. Safety is an emotive subject, and that makes it very tricky to write about, so tricky that I am almost reluctant to broach the subject at all, for fear of being branded a heretic. You may think I am advocating a lackadaisical attitude towards track day safety. Not so. However, I do feel that you need to balance the precautions against the risks.

No compromise

There are those who will countenance no compromise in safety. These safety zealots will advocate that track day cars should be prepared to motor racing safety standards with, among other things, full rollcages, full harness seat belts, race seats, external electrical cut-off switches, plumbed-in fire extinguishers and so on; and that drivers (and, presumably, their passengers) should be equipped with three-layer race suits complete with underwear, flameproof gloves and boots, full-face helmets etc. On the face of it, that may make good sense. When you see the major shunts that racing drivers not only survive, but walk away from, you might

almost argue that all road cars should be equipped with those features, and that we should all drive in full-face helmets on the road. But that would be ridiculous . . . fine in theory, perhaps, but too much of a compromise in practicality.

On the other hand there are those for whom the very appeal of track days is that you don't need all that 'bullshit'. You just turn up, plonk a helmet on your head, blast around to your heart's content all day long and then go home. For those who yearn for the freedom of the open road (sadly a thing of the past) track days are like a breath of fresh air. They afford them the opportunity and the freedom to get their jollies by driving fast, away from the obvious hazards of the public highway and without any of the stifling bureaucracy – the rules, regulations, restrictions and rigmarole – that have taken so much of the fun out of modern motor racing. Those who subscribe to this philosophy should enjoy it while they can because it may not last. (Anyone care to bet how long it will be before someone realizes there is money to be made from instituting some form of licence or permit for track day users? They could call it a non-competition licence!)

Dual purpose

Most people use some sort of road car for track day fun, so many of those motorsport-derived safety features, desirable as they might seem, can be anything from a minor

When you see a driver not only survive but in most cases walk away from a serious accident at a racing circuit, you might argue that drivers at a track day should be similarly protected by their safety equipment.

A full rollcage offers superb protection in a serious accident on the circuit, when a crash helmet is worn, but may in fact be an unwanted hazard on the road.

inconvenience to a major safety hazard *on the road*. You should be wary, therefore, that you do not make your car safer on the track but, paradoxically, more dangerous on the road, especially if you have a true dual-purpose vehicle which is inevitably going to spend more of its time on the road (arguably a more hazardous environment anyway!) than on the track.

Take the full rollcage: undoubtedly this offers a high degree of protection on the track, but this is largely predicated on you wearing a crash helmet. If you are not wearing one, it is more likely to harm you when you whack your head against it (as like as not when you are simply getting in or out of the car!), than protect you in the event of a major incident. Padding may help, but this is unlikely to guard against major impacts; it will only really protect you against minor bumps.

There is also the practical consideration that full rollcages render the back seats useless in most cars, although in some circumstances that might be considered a benefit (cue back seat driver and mother-in-law jokes!), and can even make getting in and out of the driver's seat difficult. In many cases you also have to modify the interior trim in order to fit the cage. So you need to weigh up how much you use the car

on the road, how often you need to get in and out of it and whether you need to retain access to the back seat. If you do half a dozen track days a year, but use the car for business the rest of the time, a full rollcage will soon become a major nuisance and arguably a safety hazard as well.

Spark out

Now consider the external electrical safety cut-off switch. You may be reluctant to carve holes in your vehicle's bodywork in order to fit one, especially as they are of doubtful worth: in *many* years of watching and participating in motor racing I have seldom if ever seen a fire started by an electrical short circuit that *may* have been prevented by a cut-off switch. Realistically it is a solution to a virtually non-existent problem. Of course I accept that it *could* happen, and acknowledge that the motorsports authorities need to take all reasonable precautions against all foreseeable risks; the problem arises in defining things like 'reasonable' and 'foreseeable'. In my view an electrical cut-off switch need not be considered essential for track days, especially as most modern cars have some sort of inertia switch for fuel cut-off anyway. Also, I have often mused on the nuisance value of someone

A fully plumbed-in fire extinguisher system may offer the ultimate in protection against fires, but a hand-held extinguisher is perfectly adequate, and is a useful thing to have in the car at all times.

with a modicum of knowledge of motorsport and a mischievous sense of humour removing the key when you have left the car parked somewhere!

The same goes for a plumbed-in fire extinguisher system with external handle. Think about some prankster pulling the handle when you are innocently parked in the high street! For track days, a plumbed-in system is probably a bit excessive unless you happen to have acquired a car – perhaps a 'retired' competition car – with a system already fitted. However, a portable hand-held fire extinguisher is probably a good thing to have in your car anyway. A word of warning though: if you install one make sure it cannot break free from its mountings in an accident, as it may become an unguided missile ricocheting around within the vehicle's interior, easily heavy and solid enough to cause serious or even fatal injury. At the same time you must ensure that the extinguisher is within easy reach and that whatever system is used to restrain it in its mounting is easily accessed in an emergency. This may not be an easy compromise to achieve.

Belt up

Similarly, full-harness seat belts are a great benefit on the track but a major hassle on the road. If you have never driven on the road wearing a full harness you will be amazed how often you lean forward and crane your neck to check for approaching traffic; when emerging from a staggered junction, for example. You don't think twice about this when wearing an inertia-reel belt, but you soon realize how often it happens when you are held tightly in your seat by a full harness that prevents you from doing so. The temptation is either to loosen the belts to allow you to lean forward when necessary; or alternatively to take less care at junctions, intersections, etc. It is difficult to decide which is the more dangerous!

You should also bear in mind that, strictly speaking, a 'proper' racing harness with aircraft-style turnbuckle is illegal for road use as the law requires that you should be able to fasten your seat belt with one hand. As far as I can tell this serves little purpose other than to encourage people to drive off before fastening their belts, only doing so once on the move (we've all done it!), but hey . . . far be it from me to suggest that the law is an ass.

In reality you would be very unlucky to be 'pulled' for wearing a full-harness seat belt on the road, but you might have problems if stopped for any other reason;

your 'illegal' belts might just provide the police with another stick to hit you with. They may also cause you problems at MOT test time. You can purchase full-harness systems that use a road-style buckle, which renders them road-legal, but they invariably have the shoulder straps permanently attached to the lap portion. I find these a real pain to get in and out of, especially when you are sunk into a high-sided close-fitting seat with limited 'wriggling room', and they are seldom as comfortable as a true competition harness. You might find them an acceptable compromise though.

Having said all that, a full harness and a good fitting seat are undoubtedly a great boon on the track and help you to feel 'at one' with the car. They are definitely worth having, but if you decide to fit full-harness seat belts you should retain the facility to use inertia reels on the road if at all possible.

Be reasonable
In short, while it is easy to say we should never compromise on safety, in reality some compromise is always necessary unless you are fortunate enough to have a dedicated track day vehicle, in which case I would encourage you to fit every safety feature available, budget permitting. Regrettably, however, the only way to achieve *absolute* safety is not to expose yourself to the risks of track days and fast driving in the first place. If you accept the fundamental premise, therefore, that absolute safety is not achievable, you should arrive at a *reasonable* level of safety with which you feel comfortable, and which doesn't interfere with your overall enjoyment of the car. And then drive accordingly.

The level of safety you are comfortable with will be decided largely by your approach to a track day. There are those who approach a track day as little more than a brisk drive in the country, and at the opposite extreme there are those who behave as though a track day were a major international motor race. If you want to use your day for 'a brisk drive in the country' and drive accordingly – *ie*, with a degree of restraint and caution as you would on the road – you can probably get away with the minimum of safety equipment and vehicle preparation. Okay, the unexpected can always happen, but if you always drive within your limits, with reasonable restraint, and concentrate at all times, the chances of having a serious accident are probably small; certainly no greater than when driving on the open road. An ounce of restraint is worth any amount of safety equipment. But if you are determined to push yourself and your car to the limit on every corner of every lap, then you would be wise to take greater precautions. Somewhere between those two extremes lies a happy medium that will suit your particular needs.

Head first
The one thing you cannot do without is a good crash helmet, so whatever else you do, buy the best helmet you can afford – break the budget if you have to – and never be tempted to skimp on this most important item. You may blanch at the price of a good quality helmet, but remember the old adage: the quality remains long after the price is forgotten. It is arguable whether the most expensive helmet will necessarily be the safest, as any helmet sold through legitimate channels should meet the statutory requirements for protection, but it will probably be lighter, more comfortable and more convenient to use, with for example a reliable ratchet that holds the visor in position properly, and other refinements. The models with chin spoilers and other aerodynamic features are designed for high-speed single-seater racing so are probably a bit over the top for track day use, but they do look the part, so if you can afford it . . . why not?

Once you have invested in a decent helmet it makes sense to look after it. If you have ever been to a fun karting track and used the helmets provided you will know what it is like to wear one that *hasn't* been looked after, and what a handicap a scratched or cloudy visor can be. Therefore you should always use a helmet bag (okay . . . perhaps not when you're wearing it!), not so much to protect the helmet itself as to keep the visor free from scratches. Even if you do take good care of your helmet, you will inevitably mark the visor sooner or later, so you should budget for a new visor now and then. According to the manufacturers, helmets deteriorate with age, even though the degradation is not outwardly visible, so you should also budget for helmet replacement every so often. Exactly how often you should change your helmet is impossible to say; it depends on how much you use it and how well you look after it, bearing in mind that the helmet will 'age ' even if it is not used. However, a number of institutions – the British Standards Institute and the US-based Snell Foundation foremost among them – issue standards and test helmets accordingly. Obviously you should ensure that your helmet meets the necessary standards, and ensuring your helmet meets the most recent standard is probably a reasonable guide as to how often it should be replaced.

It is a well-known fact – but I'll repeat it here anyway – that a helmet *must* be replaced, or at the very least returned to the manufacturer for inspection, after any accident. Even just dropping the helmet against a hard surface can result in damage that may not be visible to the untrained eye, so there is another argument in favour of taking good care of your headgear.

Some prefer an open-face helmet if they are driving exclusively in a closed car. However, several years ago a leading privateer touring car driver was involved in a fairly major 'shunt' and was uninjured apart from a nasty gash on the forehead inflicted, ironically, by the peak of his open-face helmet. As a helmet is supposed to prevent, not inflict injury, that incident was enough to persuade me that it is preferable to wear a full-face helmet. The debate continues, however, and I have no wish to be dogmatic about it; therefore I respect your right to make up your own mind! Of course, a full-face helmet is definitely preferable (and indeed compulsory with some track day organizers) in any sort of open car, and is therefore more versatile, so unless you

When choosing a crash helmet, buy the best you can afford – even defer your purchase if necessary – make sure it fits you properly, and look after it. It is the single most important piece of equipment you will need.

have a serious problem with claustrophobia, or some other valid objection to a full-face helmet, that is what I recommend. Also, you never know when you may be offered a ride or even a drive in an open car; at least with a full-face helmet you can take up the offer without hesitation and without having to scurry about trying to borrow a more suitable helmet. Indeed, you will probably find that if you have splashed out on a top-quality 'lid' and have become used to it, it will become very personal to you; you will be reluctant to wear anything else, and equally loathe to permit anyone else to wear it.

Suits you

Because motor manufacturers are anxious to avoid expensive litigation concerning a product liability claim, the fuel tanks of most modern cars are well protected. For that reason a modern car is unlikely to catch fire in anything less than a major accident. It is arguable, therefore, whether you really *need* to wear a race-style flameproof suit for track days, especially if you take a more casual approach to them;

If you have invested several hundred pounds in a race suit, be sure to wear it every time you take to the track. If nothing else, this will put you in the right frame of mind for driving, even if you never get to test its protective qualities.

and many don't bother. If you take things more seriously, though, and like to 'go for it', with its attendant greater risks, you should certainly wear a Nomex race suit. If you are that concerned about the fire risk, though, then in the interests of consistency you should probably also wear a balaclava, gloves and boots, as burns to the hands and feet (ever sunburnt the tops of your feet?) can be extremely painful and slow to heal. Ideally you should wear the special Nomex underwear, too, as most suits rely on the use of underwear to provide some of the insulation, and this greatly enhances their protection qualities.

The question once again is where to draw the line. Equipping yourself with all of the above could easily cost £1000 or more, and unlike, say, an expensive ski jacket, it can't really be used for anything else except perhaps the odd fancy dress party! Serious expenditure, especially if you only do a handful of track days a year. Not only that, but you also risk a serious ribbing from your mates (poser!) . . . not that you would let that influence you of course! As the chances of the car catching fire and you being unable to get out of it quickly are probably very slim, you might not think it is worthwhile to take such extreme precautions. The only thing I remain dogmatic about is if you *do* have a race suit you should always wear it, with or without the extras, as to have one and not use it, even though it may be uncomfortably hot to wear in the middle of summer, would be inexcusably foolish.

Again, if you invest upwards of £200 in a race suit it behoves you to look after it and not wear it when you need to work on the car, especially when refuelling by hand or changing the oil, as petrol and oil stains don't do much for the flame retardant properties of Nomex. Although most manufacturers recommend dry cleaning of Nomex garments I prefer gentle machine washing. It may not always look it, but driving fast is a physical activity and it is possible to work up a fair old sweat in the cockpit. In my experience(!), washing is more effective in controlling nasty niffs resulting from major deodorant failure than dry cleaning, and has no discernible ill effects.

Individual responsibility

To summarize, then, don't assume you *need* all that stuff in order to enjoy your car on the track. Track day safety is a matter of individual responsibility, and it is up to the individual to decide on a level of safety appropriate to the level of risk. Of course it is always possible to get caught out by circumstances and dumb luck (somebody 'losing it' directly in front of you, for example), but far more often circuit incidents are caused by over-confidence, fatigue, over-excitement and loss of concentration. That is why so many mishaps occur at the beginning of the day (and you can figure out for yourselves which of the above factors play a part then) and at the end (ditto!).

All of the precautions you take should be designed to enhance your own personal safety. After all, cars can always be replaced: people can not. However, you may be concerned at the financial ramifications of damaging your cherished motor car on the circuit. But don't let this put you off. Because track days are non-competitive, many insurers view them favourably, as a form of advanced driver training, and therefore it is quite possible to insure against track day mishaps, usually at quite reasonable cost. If your insurance company will not offer cover, then perhaps you should look for one that does.

Should the worst happen, for whatever reason, you can still rely to some extent on the safety features that are built into most modern cars, which may not be such a bad thing. After all, you could just as easily suffer an accident on the open road.

3

COCKPIT PREPARATION

Judging by the number of drivers I see adopting poor driving positions on track days, one of the most underrated factors in enabling you to drive both quickly and safely on the track is cockpit ergonomics.

Rakish angle

There was a time when, if you considered yourself a sporting motorist, you moved the seat rearwards as far as practicable, laid the backrest at a rakish angle and drove with your arms outstretched and head tilted back, imagining you were Jimmy Clark in the Lotus 25. As Formula One cars evolved, cockpit sides grew higher and

transparent windscreens went the way of the dodo, and it became impossible to see the driver at work, hence it was difficult to discern the driver's seating position. But as tyres grew wider and cornering speeds increased, racing cars became much more physically demanding to drive, which meant that drivers were required to sit more upright and closer to the wheel. For some reason, though, many people still tend to sit too far from the steering wheel, perhaps because they think it looks and feels 'racy'.

To understand why Clark and (later, once the other constructors had caught up

With the seminal Lotus 25, designer Colin Chapman and driver Jim Clark (seen here in the later Lotus 33 at Brands hatch) established the semi-recumbent 'lay-down' driving position which is still regarded as sporty even today, by some ill-informed enthusiasts at least.

with Lotus!) his contemporaries adopted the lay-back driving position, you have to understand the historical context. First, the ground-breaking Lotus 25 came along during the unlamented 1½-litre era of Formula One racing. These cars had little power and little grip, so they responded to a light and sensitive touch on the steering, which was possible even at full reach of the arms. For the same reasons, minimal frontal area was a critical factor in performance, so it was in Clark's interest to adopt the lay-back driving position – even though he found it uncomfortable at first – as it gave him a huge advantage. Furthermore, drivers in those days still used open-face helmets and goggles, so Clark was able to tilt his head back and peer down his nose more or less without impediment. He might have found it much harder to adapt had full-face helmets been in vogue then, as he would almost certainly have found the lower portion of the helmet encroaching on his line of vision.

So what was right for Clark in 1964 is not necessarily right for you in the 21st century. You simply cannot steer with sufficient accuracy if your arms are at full reach. Perversely, many women pose the opposite problem. It is a generalization, but none the less valid for that, that they tend to sit too close to the steering wheel, maybe because often they are shorter and find that the only way they can operate the pedals properly is to have the seat well forward, which then puts them too close to the wheel. Then again, some seem genuinely to prefer to sit up close, perhaps because this instils a greater feeling of control. But paradoxically it could well make things more difficult for them, as it is impossible to control a car if your arms are too cramped to allow you to steer properly. Either way it is worth going to a good deal of trouble to establish a comfortable seating position. So how do you go about this?

Get down

You should start by locating the seat as low as practicable. In road driving you need to be seated reasonably high to judge your proximity to other vehicles, especially when parking. Hopefully you won't be looking for a parking space on the circuit, so you can afford to sit lower than you might in road driving. If you have height-adjustable seats this is easy, but if you have seats of fixed height you will have to reach some sort of compromise (you'll notice that word crops up a lot!) if you regularly use the car on the road as well. Within reason, you can't sit too low for track use, bearing in mind that you don't need to see the road immediately in front of you. If you sit lower in the car than you are accustomed to, you may find placing the car accurately is difficult at first, but it will become easier with time. Even if it feels alien and strange at first it is worth persevering with a low seating position as it lowers the centre of gravity and makes you feel you are sitting in, rather than on, the car.

When you have the seat height to your liking, move the seat forward and back on its runners until you can comfortably operate the pedals. In more upmarket vehicles with multi-adjustable seats you may also be able to adjust the angle of the seat squab, but this may involve some trade-off between angle and reach to the pedals. It is important that you can fully disengage the clutch without stretching; if you achieve that, safe operation of the brakes and accelerator should automatically follow.

When you are happy that the squab is in the right place you can tilt the backrest to give you the right reach to the steering wheel or, if the steering wheel is adjustable for reach, at a comfortable angle. Don't be tempted to recline the backrest too much. You need to be relaxed, but you must also be alert, and there is a difference between being relaxed and slumping behind the wheel.

Steering reach

Once you have the backrest angle to your liking, adjust the wheel for reach. This is perhaps the single most important factor, and a good rule of thumb is to be able to place the inside of your wrist on the top of the steering wheel rim without stretching, while firmly belted in. If the reach to the wheel is not adjustable you may need to juggle the squab position and backrest

When seated and strapped in normally, you should be able to place the inside of your wrist on the top of the steering wheel rim without stretching.

This will result in a relaxed yet alert posture. When grasping the steering wheel normally, your arms should be comfortably bent, you should be close enough to allow good leverage, but not so close as to inhibit full and natural rotation of the wheel.

angle to achieve the best compromise between reach to the pedals and to the steering wheel. In the unlikely event that you cannot get it right, you might need to reach for the toolbox instead; it may be possible to fit spacers to either the steering wheel or the pedals, depending on the nature of the problem.

The height of the steering wheel is arguably the least important factor inasmuch as most people can tolerate a good deal of variation in wheel height without undue discomfort. Even though you might prefer it to be slightly higher or lower, it doesn't impair your ability to steer. If the wheel is adjustable for height you can simply experiment to find the position that best suits you. With your

hands on the wheel at ten-to-two, or quarter-to-three if you prefer, your arms should be relaxed, with elbows comfortably bent. If your arms become fatigued after a number of laps you may have the wheel too high or be sitting too far away. You might not be aware that you are becoming tired, but you will probably tend to grasp the bottom half of the wheel and feed it through your hands rather than maintaining your grip over the top half of the wheel (more on this in *Steering Techniques*).

I like to be able to see the top of the steering wheel rim in my peripheral vision, just below the line of sight, although this is not essential. If the wheel is too low, however, your hands may foul on the tops of your thighs when you need to apply a lot of

It is remarkable how much a top-quality leather-bound steering wheel can contribute to your feeling of control, especially when the size is appropriate. You should avoid the temptation to choose too small a wheel. Momo steering wheels, as seen here, are among the best.

lock, or the bottom of the wheel may catch your thighs and interfere with proper operation of the pedals. However, this is unlikely to happen if you have chosen a suitably low seat position as I suggest.

Size matters

Another important factor is the size of the steering wheel, which influences both the positioning of the wheel and the amount of effort required to steer. It can also have a major influence on how easy it is to get into and out of the car, especially one with a small cockpit (Caterham Seven, for instance) or door opening (Lotus Elise with the 'hood' erected, for example), or when a high-sided seat and/or a full rollcage with door intrusion bars makes entry and exit difficult. In such cases a single-seater-style detachable steering wheel can be used to good effect.

There is a tendency, again probably because people think it 'racy', to use too small a steering wheel, but this can make the car feel as though it is steering you rather than the other way round, a sensation I have never particularly enjoyed! In order to maintain full steering control and, equally important, to *feel* in control, you need a reasonable-sized wheel. It is impossible to specify an optimum size to suit every case as this will depend on the steering weight and speed, the amount of lock available and, to a great extent, personal preference, but I would counsel against going too small.

I should mention at this point the difference a good steering wheel can make to your driving enjoyment. Viewed objectively a steering wheel shouldn't make any difference, and certainly the benefits cannot be measured or quantified, but I find that a nice stitched leather-bound wheel with a chunky rim can enhance the driving experience by providing superior grip and a greater feeling of control.

Nowadays few aftermarket 'sports' steering wheels have a simple round-section rim; many have an oval section, which may fit the hands more comfortably, and most feature some sort of shaping in the handhold area. These shaped areas can be extremely useful in helping you to

return to the straight-ahead position if you have been forced to relinquish your grip. Although suede may seem a good covering material as it offers more grip than smooth leather, it quickly wears smooth and loses any initial advantage; it also very quickly looks tatty, so a nice matt leather is a better bet. For some reason the best steering wheels come from Italy, Nardi, Personal and Momo being the pick of the crop. Even if the benefits are purely psychological, who says that is not worthwhile? It might not help you drive any better, but it sure feels like it does. In my view, a good steering wheel is an investment in driving pleasure and satisfaction.

Seat of learning

Competition seats offer certain advantages in that they have fewer adjustments, hence there are fewer variables and therefore less scope for confusion and indecision. The angle of the seatback to the squab, for example, is fixed. By the same token, though, because it is not so easy to change things once the seat is bolted in place, it becomes more crucial to get the initial adjustments right.

Most competition seats are mounted on plates that incorporate a multitude of alternative mounting holes. In principle you should follow the sequence described above: start by mounting the seat as low as practicable, then adjust the reach to the pedals. If you are setting up a fixed seat on mounting brackets with multiple holes you can also experiment with the mounting angle of the seat. Most aftermarket competition-style bucket seats have a relatively upright backrest and, if mounted 'level' (*ie* if you use the same numbered mounting hole front and back), may make you feel as if you are sliding or falling forward out of the seat. If so you should raise the front and/or lower the rear of the seat, which will recline the backrest more and raise the front of the squab, giving greater support for your thighs. Don't go too far, though, else you may find it difficult to operate the pedals properly as you will be pushing against the seat squab and trying to compress the foam with the underside of your thigh. You may need to juggle the

Competition seats come in all shapes and sizes to suit all shapes and sizes. Mounting brackets usually come drilled with multiple holes for maximum versatility, but considerable care is needed in mounting, especially with a fixed seatback angle, to obtain the right angle of recline.

height, reach and rake of the seat until you find the position that is right for you. As always, it is a matter of finding the right compromise.

In fact competition seats can be a mixed blessing in a true dual-purpose road and track day vehicle, especially if they are permanently fixed. With their high sides and buttock-clenching dimensions they undoubtedly offer more support, and for that reason may give the driver greater rapport with the vehicle. But they are also much harder to get into and out of, especially if you are clambering in past a full rollcage with side intrusion bars. Furthermore, losing the tilt-and-slide facility may render access to the back seat difficult, if not impossible, while bolting the seat firmly in place – although it may arguably offer greater safety – also means that it could be difficult for anyone else to drive the car. That contingency may seldom arise, but there may come a time when you wish to sell, for example, when any intending purchaser will almost certainly insist on a test drive.

It is also questionable whether being 'clamped' in the one position for any length of time is a good thing. Conventional production car seats at least allow you to

move about and adjust your position slightly from time to time, which helps to maintain comfort and reduce fatigue on a long journey. Giving due consideration to all the compromises required, a competition 'bucket ' fixed to the standard seat runners, which would at least allow some fore-and-aft adjustment, may be a good solution.

Pedal power

Ideally, the placement of the pedals should allow you to move your right foot rapidly and accurately between brake and accelerator, and to heel-and-toe when changing gear. This is an advanced driving technique, which allows you to better synchronize your gearchanges when changing down under braking. We'll come back to that later. However, in order to expedite this the brake and accelerator pedals should be arranged with the accelerator pedal lower than the brake pedal, so that they are at the same height – or very nearly so – when the brakes are applied hard. They should also be close enough together that you can operate both pedals at once by straddling them with your right foot.

Because most vehicle manufacturers

nowadays understand these requirements, the pedal placement in most 'sporty' cars is satisfactory, if not quite perfect in every case. If not, you may have to make some adjustments. Often the accelerator pedal and cable arrangement will have a stop at either end to limit travel and prevent stretching of the cable, and it may be possible to adjust these stops to provide a stroke at the pedal that better matches the position of the brake pedal when fully depressed. Before making any adjustments, however, it is worth checking that the braking system is working perfectly, and in particular that there is no air in the system making the brake pedal 'soft'. Similarly, it may be possible to adjust the lateral (side-to-side) placement of the pedals to allow easier heel-and-toe operation. Depending on your mechanical aptitude, though, it may be better to leave such adjustments to the experts. An easier option may be to use aftermarket pedal pads, which are available from a number of 'performance parts' manufacturers. Usually they are drilled and anodized in fancy colours, and while they are usually considered a cosmetic item, they can have their uses.

As a very last resort, you may be able to bend one or more of the pedals to suit. Usually, the accelerator pedal will be of lighter, flimsier construction than the brake pedal, and may therefore better lend itself to a gentle 'tweak'. If you must bend the brake pedal, it may behove you to engage a professional metal fabricator as it is obviously imperative that you do not weaken this safety-critical component.

Another important feature is an effective clutch footrest. You will probably find that when cornering hard you have to brace yourself against centrifugal force, and being able to brace your clutch foot against the floor or transmission tunnel is most useful. Clearly you should avoid resting your foot on the clutch pedal, as in hard cornering it is difficult to avoid inadvertently applying pressure to the pedal, causing clutch slip and overheating. Like pedal pads, a clutch footrest can be obtained from various purveyors of performance 'goodies', but it is a relatively simple item and could be easily fabricated.

Compromise

As you may have realized by now, all the factors that go to make a safe and comfortable driving environment are interrelated. There are a multitude of adjustments to be made: the height and angle of the seat squab; the distance from the pedals; the angle of the backrest; and the size, height, angle and reach to the steering wheel. Depending on which adjustments are available to you, you may have to be prepared for a certain amount of to-ing and fro-ing before you arrive at the best compromise (that word again). Beware that what feels right in the workshop may not feel right on the circuit as it is difficult to simulate actually driving the car. You may need several attempts to get it right.

Buckling down

Once you are sitting comfortably it is time to adjust the seat belts to suit. If you are using a reasonably standard road car with an inertia-reel belt you may not have any worthwhile adjustment available. The best thing in this case is not to use the seat belt (no, I don't mean you shouldn't *wear* it, I just hope you don't need to *use* it!). Notwithstanding my earlier comments (see *Safety Fast*) on the disadvantages of full four- or six-point harnesses, being strapped firmly in place in a supportive seat will give you a much better feel for the car. As I suggested, if you use your track day car on the road you really should retain the inertia-reel seat belts, but full-harness belts are a worthwhile addition.

When using a full-harness seat belt it is vitally important that the lap portion of the belt rests over your pelvic bones, not over your abdomen. An inertia-reel belt keeps the lap portion tensioned over your pelvic (hip) bones automatically . . . or should do. If it doesn't, this is another argument in favour of fitting a full harness. However, it is crucial that full-harness belts are mounted and adjusted correctly. It is all too easy to incorrectly adjust a full harness so that the lap portion rides up above your hip bones and over your abdomen. This is highly undesirable as not only does it not

The lap portion of the full harness should be kept as low as possible so any strain or impact is taken on the pelvic (hip) bones (right), and not on the soft parts of the abdomen (left).

restrain you properly because your abdomen is all soft tissue (some softer than others!), but you also run the risk of internal injuries; your hip bones are strong, but your vital internal organs are not.

The problem is that tightening the shoulder straps automatically pulls on the lap belt, so the lap portion has to be very tight – almost to the point of discomfort – in order to resist this upward pull. Correct mounting of the lap belt is important. Clearly it is preferable to have the belts mounted both correctly and comfortably tight, rather than having to wear them uncomfortably tight in order to overcome a problem caused by poor location. If the anchorage points are too far behind the seat the action of tightening the shoulder straps exerts an even greater upwards pull. Ideally, therefore, the lap belt should be as short as practicable and mounted as near to your hips as possible. If you like, think in terms of the lap belt holding you *down* in the seat and the shoulder straps holding

you *back*: the more you rely on the lap belt holding you back and the shoulder straps holding you down, the more problem you will have with the lap portion riding up. If the mountings are well behind you when you are seated normally, if possible you should consider relocating them further forward.

Ideally, the angle of the shoulder strap when it passes over your shoulder should be as near as practicable to 90deg. If you are preparing a production car for track days, however, and are unwilling to make major alterations, you may prefer to use or adapt the existing seat belt anchorages. This has certain advantages inasmuch as you can be confident they are man enough for the job. Clearly all seat belt anchorages must be engineered to withstand substantial loads, and if you are not competent to deal with installing them you should seek expert guidance. If you stick with the standard anchorage, though, and find they are not ideally located, there may be little alternative but to use the dreaded crutch straps as well.

These are designed to prevent you sliding forward underneath the lap belt in a severe frontal impact, particularly in a very low sports car or single-seater with a reclined seating position. Although crutch straps are regarded as indispensable in all serious racing cars, many drivers also view them with suspicion . . . for obvious reasons. In a normal saloon or sports car, with a reasonably upright seating position, sliding out from underneath the lap belts — otherwise known as submarining — is unlikely, especially if the lap belt is kept short and tight and worn low over the hips. However, crutch straps do have another advantage in that they usually attach to the buckle and hold the lap portion of the belt in place, resisting the upward pull of the shoulder straps. Therefore they can have their uses, even in a saloon car where the risk of submarining may be minimal.

Because it is important to have the lap portion of the belt tight you should secure and adjust this first. The crutch straps, if fitted, can then be secured. Usually crutch straps are of a fixed length, which is adjusted on installation and can only be altered by partially dismantling them. Therefore it may take some fiddling to get the lengths right at the installation stage, but they shouldn't need adjusting thereafter (there's probably a joke in there somewhere, but I won't go there!). Because crutch straps are designed and intended to help the main harness hold you in place they don't have to be done up quite as tightly . . . which is a relief. If you are suffering any discomfort from your crutch straps you can probably afford to ease them off a little, although of course they shouldn't be loose. As with most other aspects of getting the cockpit set up perfectly for you, there may be some trial-and-error involved, and a certain amount of perseverance may be needed.

The final step in installing yourself is to plug in the shoulder straps and pull them tight. The lap belt and shoulder straps should be adjusted to just this side of discomfort, at which point you should be barely able to move. If the belts are too loose you risk injury from impact with them when the slack is taken up in an accident. Being tightly strapped in should also make you feel part of the car and give you a better feel for it. So in terms of safety, and in the pleasure and satisfaction you get from track days, taking the time and trouble to sort out your driving environment will repay you handsomely.

In the days when Juan Manuel Fangio and his contemporaries drove cars like the Alfa Romeo 159, grip was limited, and tyre failure was an ever present hazard.

4

TYRE CARE

One of the first things you will learn when you start to do track days is the importance of tyre pressures. In the old days, when Fangio and Co raced their front-engined dinosaurs on spindly wire wheels, their tyres were narrow and tall, with carcasses manufactured largely from natural products, like cotton for the belts and carcass reinforcement and natural rubber for the tread and sidewalls. Tyres were widely regarded as the weak link; they had little grip, yet nevertheless they wore quickly and were dangerously prone to failure, throwing treads or blowing out, with exasperating and sometimes tragic results.

Cotton and rubber
Because of the limitations of cotton and natural rubber as constructional materials, the sidewalls were inherently rather flexible, and in order to reduce flexing the tyres were routinely inflated to 50 or 60psi, or perhaps even more. This served to stabilize the carcass and made for more progressive and predictable handling; it also helped to minimize tread squirm, often the cause of overheating of the tread, loss of grip and, in extreme cases, tyre failure. It probably also meant that the tyre tread took on a slightly convex profile so that most of the time only the central portion of the tread was in proper contact with the road, but this was not necessarily a bad thing as suspension geometry was

improperly understood in those days and at least it meant that control of camber angles was not so critical. The tyre was also less likely to roll off the rim if the wheel went into positive camber, as usually happens with parallel equal-length wishbones, a common design feature at the time. Whatever, the plusses (of high inflation pressures) outweighed the minuses.

Brains
In those days going faster usually involved screwing in a bigger, more powerful motor, but in the early 1960s the best racing brains in the business (with Colin Chapman of Lotus playing a prominent role) began to realize the importance of roadholding, and as a wide tyre could offer more grip than a narrow one, tyres began to grow inexorably wider. This coincided with the development of greatly improved materials for tyre manufacture: synthetic rubber, and nylon (rayon) belts for tread and sidewall reinforcement. Indeed, it is arguable which came first: the realization that wider tyres could produce more grip and hence improved roadholding; or the means to produce them.

Tyres didn't merely become bigger, however. At the same time sidewalls were made shallower so that aspect (height:width) ratios went through 70, 60, then 50% and even lower; and so the modern wide low-profile tyre was born. Shallower sidewalls are obviously more

rigid; therefore it was no longer necessary to use high inflation pressures in order to maintain carcass rigidity, and with lower pressures the tread became more compliant and so better able to conform to irregularities in the road. At the same time tread widths became much wider. However, a wider tyre is of little value if only a small portion of the tread is in contact with the road surface, so in order to make the most of that larger contact patch it became much more important to optimize inflation pressures and suspension geometry, in particular camber angles. Ever since then, the emphasis in motor racing has been on improving roadholding and increasing cornering speeds. Tyres have been improved continuously, and there is little doubt that the driver of even an average road car today has more tyre grip available than a Grand Prix driver of the '50s.

Inflationary pressure

Typically, modern high-performance tyres with aspect ratios in the 40-60% range have reasonably stiff sidewalls, so do not have to be over-inflated in order to stabilize the carcass. However, the manufacturers will always allow some sidewall flex in the interests of ride comfort, therefore some increase in the tyre pressures recommended for the road should be considered; I would suggest experimenting in the range 0-10psi above standard. As a general rule heavier cars should have their tyre pressures increased more than lighter ones; indeed some lightweights like the Caterham Seven can perform perfectly satisfactorily on track using standard road pressures.

Bear in mind also that as the tyres become hot the air inside them expands, which increases the pressure. The only reason to be aware of this is to ensure that you are consistent, and always measure

A Caterham Seven remains a popular choice for track days. Although they look great on 15in wheels and tyres, best performance is usually to be found with 13in wheels.

tyre pressure either 'hot' or 'cold'. If you always measure pressures cold, the hot pressures may well be 5-10psi higher, but that doesn't really matter. Alternatively, you may prefer to measure tyre pressures hot, in which case you should do several fast laps, then measure pressure as soon as practicable after returning to the pits or paddock, and bleed off the excess pressure built up if necessary.

The increase in pressure is actually due to the moisture content of the air within the tyre, and it is possible to minimize unwanted pressure build-up by using nitrogen, or specially-prepared 'dry' air – available through some specialist tyre outlets – to inflate the tyres. However, for all but the most serious, this is probably more trouble that it is worth, and indeed, for the average track day driver, without a pit crew to help, it is probably easier just to monitor tyre pressures cold. Whichever option you choose, don't forget to return your tyres to normal road pressures before driving home.

Heat

Tyres work best within a specific operating temperature range, although for high-performance road tyres this is usually fairly broad, so a considerable tolerance and hence a substantial safety margin is built in. Therefore you should try to optimize static camber angles and tyre pressures so as to keep the tread square to the road with as even as possible contact pressure across the tyre contact patch, which will enable the tyre to reach and maintain its optimum operating temperature.

Heat, though, is the tyres' sworn enemy. Excessive heat will cause loss of performance and rapid tread wear. Presupposing that the tyre is appropriate to the size, weight and performance of the vehicle to which it is fitted (*ie* it is not simply overloaded), overheating may be caused by over- or under-inflation, or unfavourable suspension geometry, causing the tyre to run on a fairly narrow strip of tread instead of its full width. Heat build-up in the tyre tends to be concentrated where the material is thickest. Usually, this will be in the shoulders which, as Sod's Law would have it, take the most abuse in hard cornering anyway, especially if you have a lot of body roll and the heavily loaded outside front wheel adopts a positive camber angle, causing the tyre to tuck-under. You should inspect the tyres regularly, therefore, and be particularly vigilant for any signs of chunking or overheating in the shoulder area, especially if you are driving your car on track for the first time.

Squirm

Tread squirm, when the tread blocks move about under the influence of severe cornering forces, can also lead to overheating. It should be self-evident that this is worst when the tyres are new, when the unsupported tread blocks are tallest. Brand new tyres may initially appear to have a horrendous wear rate when used on the track, but this will usually stabilize unless they are seriously abused. Indeed, some high-performance road tyres are actually manufactured with a greatly reduced tread depth (approximately 4mm when new), which largely eradicates the problem of tread squirm, although in reality they are usually thinly disguised race tyres intended for motorsport categories which require 'road' tyres. They may also be of a special soft compound offering considerably greater grip in exchange for a substantially higher wear rate. It is probably advisable, therefore, to avoid using these on the road.

So it is best to use part-worn tyres on the track and certainly to avoid going to the track with brand new tyres. However, if you use you track day car on the road, at some stage you will presumably be forced to fit new tyres. If you have no option but to use new(ish) tyres on a track day, at least try to treat them gently to begin with, and inspect them periodically for overheating or other signs of distress. Some tyre outlets that specialize in supplying tyres for motorsport can offer a 'buffing' service, which can take new tyres down to a tread depth of 4-5mm. Tyres so treated will offer considerably better grip and may be less inclined to overheat, but you may resent the loss of the first few thousand miles-worth of tread, and in reality this is probably wasteful for track days where – in theory at least – you are probably not concerned at screwing the last tenth out of your car on every lap.

Another factor to beware of is that part-worn tyres will not cut through standing water as well as full-tread tyres, so you run a greater risk of aquaplaning; exercise caution, therefore, if you encounter a wet track at any track day. For obvious reasons you should also beware of using well-worn tyres on the road. If you drive to a track day with tyres that are barely legal, after a hard day at the track they will almost certainly be well below the legal tread depth. The tyres will usually work best – on a dry track at least – when the tread is all but worn out, so if it is practicable to do so, you may consider maintaining a spare set of wheels with part-worn or 'race' tyres for use specifically on the track.

Geometry lessons

The static suspension geometry plays a major role in obtaining the best grip and wear from the tyres. Because body roll in cornering tends to play havoc with the suspension geometry some compromise will usually be called for. For example, if you get a lot of positive camber on the outside front wheel in hard cornering, which is fairly common, you will probably get a lot of understeer, which if you just press on regardless will very quickly tear up the outside shoulder due to local overheating. It is especially galling to have to scrap a tyre because the outside shoulder is below the legal minimum tread depth when the bulk of the tread may be virtually intact.

Most cars adopt some positive camber in roll, so in order to keep the wheel upright and the tyre square to the road in hard cornering you may have to give the wheel some negative camber in the static condition. But if you find you need a lot of static negative camber (more than about 2½deg negative, say) on the front wheels due to excessive body roll, this can lead to uncertain straight-line stability, especially

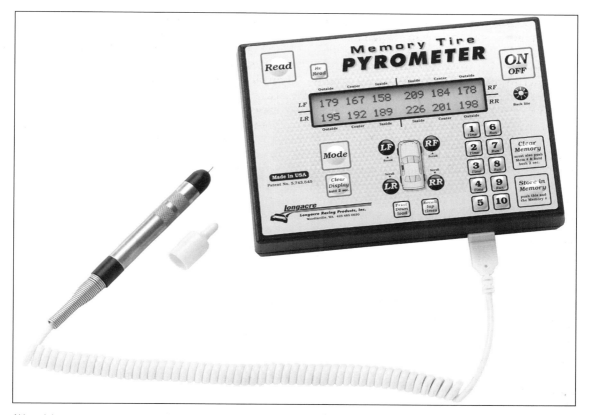

Although it may seem an extravagance, a tyre pyrometer will help you establish the optimum tyre pressures and suspension geometry. This could save you money in the long run in the form of reduced tyre wear.

under heavy braking, when nosedive can induce even more negative camber, while on the road the tyre will spend a lot of time running on the inside shoulder and will suffer rapid wear. It is only under the hard cornering achievable on track that the camber angle will be optimized. In this case you should probably consider some measure to reduce body roll: lowering the car, firmer springs, stiffer anti-roll bars, or some combination of these measures.

If you are using your road car on track days, once again you may need to compromise somewhat. When you have too much negative camber on the road you can wear out the inside shoulders of the tyres prematurely, but if you have too little negative camber you will wear out the outside shoulders on the track. There are a lot of factors to juggle, and it may prove difficult to reconcile them all.

The easiest way to measure whether the tyre has the optimum pressure and camber angle when cornering is to monitor the temperature across the tread, using a device called a tyre pyrometer. Unfortunately these tend to be moderately expensive and are not much good for anything else, so investing in one might seem an extravagance. It may be worth considering, though, especially if you can share the cost among several fellow enthusiasts. Indeed, it could actually save you money as on a large, heavy and powerful car you could destroy a set of tyres in a day if the wear pattern is particularly disadvantageous.

If you do manage to buy, borrow or blag a tyre pyrometer and go testing with it, it is important to work in a logical and methodical way, recording tyre temperatures as soon as possible (before the tyre is able to cool down) every time you stop in the pits. Ideally, you should measure at three points across the tread, and your aim should be to obtain as near as possible equal temperatures. If the centre of the tread is getting hot the tyre is over-inflated, if only the outer portion of tread is too hot you could probably use a little more negative camber and . . . well, it's pretty much commonsense, really, provided you take your time and think it through.

Of course all of the above presupposes that you are able to adjust suspension geometry at will, which may not always be the case. If not you will need to compromise (that word again!): either by accepting the vehicle's limitations and slowing down; accepting excessive tyre wear; or perhaps by modifying the vehicle to allow more suspension adjustment. It really is difficult to have a truly versatile car suitable for both general road use and track days, so you need to decide whether you can live

with a little less comfort, practicality or whatever, on the road in order to enjoy more track performance, or vice versa. The nearest thing to a true multi-purpose vehicle is a Caterham Seven, but even that is not to everyone's taste and may be too much of a compromise (in comfort, weather protection, luggage capacity, etc) for some.

It is sobering to reflect that when you are conducting a ton or more of metal, rubber, plastic, leather and who knows what else – not to mention precious bodily parts – at 100mph or more, your sole contact with *terra firma* is through those four tiny patches of rubber, each little larger than your handprint. It is obvious, therefore, that tyres have a vital role to play; look after them, and they will look after you.

If you arrive at a track day with brand new tyres their initial wear rate will be horrendous due to excessive heat build-up. Handling may also be compromised due to tread squirm. Far better to use part-worn tyres, but remember they must still be legal for the drive home at the end of the day.

5

BRAKE CARE AND COOLING

Virtually all modern cars are equipped with adequate brakes for road use. By adequate I mean that the vehicle's brakes should be capable of overcoming the tractive capabilities of the tyres (*ie* locking the wheels) at any speed the vehicle can reach. It would be astonishing if any modern production car were delivered with brakes that couldn't meet this criterion. But are brakes that may be perfectly satisfactory on the road adequate for track use?

Potential

Usually this will depend on the performance potential of the car. You would have thought that a high-performance saloon or sports car would have brakes designed to withstand the rigours of repeated high-speed stops, whereas a small economy hatchback, with no performance pretensions whatever, might struggle to cope with the demands of circuit braking. In fact the reverse is often the case. Because its top speed is modest (110mph, say) and it takes some time to achieve it, the economy hatchback will usually have more than adequate brakes whereas those on a high-performance saloon or sports car may be found wanting in repeated hard use. It is obviously more difficult to slow a car to 50mph from 150mph than from 100mph, especially as the faster car will almost invariably also be heavier. The problem is likely to be dispersing the heat

build-up caused by repeated heavy braking.

Brakes work by converting kinetic energy (in the form of motion) into thermal energy (heat). You can actually calculate how much heat is generated, but this is no place for complicated formulae; suffice to say that it is a *phenomenal* amount of heat. In order to work efficiently brakes need to operate within a specific temperature range, usually dictated by the optimum working temperature of the friction (pad) material. It should be apparent that the faster and heavier the car, the more heat will be generated under braking. The shedding of this heat constitutes the greatest challenge to the brake designer.

Fade

From the driver's seat you will know the brakes have overheated when you experience a phenomenon known as brake fade. This occurs when the friction material exceeds its optimum operating temperature range, so the pads no longer clamp the discs effectively, or in some cases when the hydraulic brake fluid boils and the pressure you apply at the pedal is not transferred to the pads. The bubbles formed during boiling of the fluid are compressible, so when you press the pedal you are merely compressing the air in the fluid rather than pressing the pads against the disc; this is what gives overheated brakes their characteristic spongy pedal feel. If fade is the result of overheated pad material the brakes will usually recover if allowed to cool gradually, but in the latter case the pedal will remain spongy because of the bubbles trapped in the system, which will have to be bled to purge the aerated fluid. Unless some provision is made to conduct cooling air to the brakes this is likely to recur, so regular bleeding may prove necessary.

This is a good policy in any event as brake fluid is hygroscopic: that is, it absorbs water. Over a period of time the moisture content in the fluid builds up and this lowers the fluid's boiling point – usually around 550degF – making brake fade much more likely. If you bleed the brakes regularly this problem is much reduced as old fluid is purged from the system and fresh fluid introduced each time. If you don't find it necessary to bleed the brakes regularly, though, it is still advisable to replace the fluid annually to maintain its boiling point.

Silicon brake fluid is not hygroscopic and therefore maintains its optimum boiling point over a far longer period – indefinitely if the advertising claims are to be believed – and unlike conventional brake fluid it will not attack your paintwork if spilled. You would have thought with those advantages silicone brake fluid would have taken over from conventional fluids, but for reasons that are not entirely clear it has not gained widespread acceptance. It is a little more expensive, but nothing like as costly as top-of-the-range competition fluids. However, it should not be mixed with conventional brake fluid, and as it is not widely available for sale you should always carry some in the car in case you need to top up.

If you are lucky, brake fade will occur progressively, giving you some warning of impending problems. In its mildest form you will notice that for a given pedal pressure you are slowing down less; or for a given rate of retardation you are required to press the pedal harder. Of course, if you are already braking at the last possible moment this loss in braking efficiency can cause you a nasty moment as you will arrive at the turn-in point still carrying too much speed. You may have to do some

They are not called hot laps for nothing! After a series of fast laps, you should do a gentle lap – or even two – in order to allow hard-worked machinery to cool down gradually. This will avoid the phenomenon of heat soak. To avoid 'cooking' the brakes, you should always leave the car in gear, or chock a wheel if necessary.

pretty fancy steering to keep from sliding wide, spinning, or even going off the road altogether!

So you should be alert to this sensation, and if it happens, gratefully accept it as a warning that the brakes are getting too hot, and ease off. Whereas if you were racing, determination, pride and a sense of obligation to your team or sponsor might compel you to try to nurse the brakes to the end of the race, on a track day there is no compulsion to continue. If you simply press on regardless you will experience severe fade, which feels virtually the same as total brake failure because pressure on the pedal has no discernible effect; clearly, if that happens unexpectedly you may need some luck to avoid an accident.

Cool down
However, if you start to experience brake fade and wisely decide to stop, don't just go straight back to the pits and switch off. Complete a lap or two at low speed, without using the brakes at all if possible, and allow

the air circulating around them to cool them gradually. This will avoid the phenomenon of heat soak. If you simply stop when all the brake components are still red-hot, more heat will be conducted away into the surrounding components rather than radiated harmlessly away by the air. In the severest cases, heat soak when stationary can boil the brake fluid, melt the grease in the wheel bearings, destroy rubber seals and even set fire to the brake pads.

Once you are back at the pits, on no account sit with your foot on the brake, and avoid using the handbrake. If the pads are allowed to touch the discs when you are stationary, the heat trapped where the two materials are in contact can easily distort the disc, or even fuse the pad to it. Usually you will experience this as a vibration under braking next time out. If you are very lucky it could be just a bit of pad material torn away when you moved off, in which case it will usually be scraped off as the brakes are applied, and the vibration will go away; but if the disc is distorted it will

not recover and may be reduced to scrap. It may be advisable to gently roll the car back and forth for a few moments after you stop to avoid creating hot spots, and if you need to prevent it from rolling away when parked in the pits, leave it in gear, or chock a wheel.

However, it is better to have cooled the brakes before you come to a halt, which is always good policy whenever you have completed a number of fast laps, and not just when you sense that fade may be imminent. Those cool-down laps will keep the brakes working better for longer, and greatly extend the life of all your brake components.

Speed range
You might suppose that the manufacturers of fast road cars would slap on the biggest, most powerful brakes that will fit inside the wheel rims and that these will easily prove adequate for track use too. Sadly, life is not that simple. A fast, heavy car, even if it has a top speed of 150mph or more, will spend much of its time operating in the

Porsche always seems to be able to provide its customers with fabulous brakes, one of the many reasons why Porsches are a popular track day weapon.

same speed range as the economy hatchback, ie 0-100mph or even less. So while it must be capable of braking safely from top speed, it is just as important that its brakes should work satisfactorily at low speed, as a result of which the brakes on many high-performance cars are a little on the small side for track use. Whilst they will easily shrug off the effects of a standard fade test or an emergency stop, they may not be able to withstand the effect of repeated hard stops from high speed, bearing in mind that on a typical track day you could be doing the equivalent of an emergency stop from very high speed several times every lap. Let's face it, if you were habitually doing this on the road, you should be asking yourself some serious questions about your style of driving!

Glazed expression

The problem is that in normal road use oversize brakes will seldom if ever get up to temperature, and that brings its own problems. When you are trundling around town at low speed the brakes are likely to need a hefty shove on the pedal, and because they seldom get up to proper operating temperature they may be inclined to glaze the pads. For those unfamiliar with this phenomenon it is just what it sounds like. If the pads are only ever applied lightly and the pad material never gets thoroughly warmed through, a hard skin or glaze builds up on the friction surface and the pads lose all their abrasiveness or 'bite'. This in turn may result in a lot of unseemly noises, squeals, graunches and so on, which are likely to dismay the owners of fast, expensive cars. Big brakes also tend to be heavier and more expensive, so for all those reasons the manufacturers usually specify the smallest brakes they can reasonably get away with. There is no criticism implied in this, as we must recognize that even the manufacturers of fast and expensive cars need to compromise.

The higher the car's top speed the more difficult it becomes for the manufacturer to arrive at a compromise that will satisfy everyone, but Porsche seems able to resolve this, so it is not for nothing that Porsches

are a popular choice for track day enthusiasts. But this may be at least partly because people *expect* Porsches to have fabulous brakes and they are prepared to put up with higher pedal pressures, and maybe a little bit of squealing or graunching at low speed, as the penalty for superb track day braking. Nor should we overlook the fact that Porsches are relatively expensive to buy and maintain, but nevertheless it must be conceded that virtually all Porsches have fabulous brakes, which are well able to withstand the rigours of track day use.

Upgrade

Because of the compromises inherent in a road car's braking system, you may decide to upgrade the brakes for track use. Undoubtedly the simplest upgrade is high-performance brake pads, which may be fitted without any other modifications. Some manufacturers and suppliers talk in terms of 'hard' and 'soft' pads. As a rule, soft pads will have a higher coefficient of friction, a lower resistance to temperature and probably a greater wear rate. Therefore they will be easier to bed in; they will offer good initial bite and be easy to modulate even when cold; and they will resist glazing. For those reasons, most production cars are fitted as standard with relatively soft pads. They may however be less resistant to high temperatures, and consequently prone to fade under extreme conditions. Harder pads will need careful bedding in; may not work well until warm; may require higher pedal pressures and be less sensitive to modulation; and may be prone to glazing. However, they will be much more resistant to high temperatures.

You may be tempted to assume that because the front brakes do the majority of the work, fitting upgraded pads to the front only would be a good solution, but you should be wary. This may upset the front-to-rear brake balance; even worse, the balance may alter with brake temperature as the performance characteristics of the front and rear pads will be different, with different rates of warm-up. The rears may lock first when the brakes are cold, for example, and the fronts once they are hot, or *vice versa*. This will lead to highly unpredictable brake response, and although in theory you shouldn't lock the brakes unless you have made a mistake, nevertheless you need the brakes to be on your side when you *do* make one – as most of us do at some time or other – or in an emergency. Premature brake locking at one end or the other is extremely difficult for even the most highly skilled drivers to contend with. Whenever possible, therefore, you should use the same friction material front and rear.

When you weigh up the pros and cons of hard *versus* soft pads, it should be apparent that you should use the softest pads that provide the necessary resistance to fade. However, some pads seem to break the rules, especially the latest composite types, described as Kevlar, carbon metallic, and so forth. They can sometimes offer the advantages of soft pads with the temperature resistance of hard pads, although there will usually be a price to pay in terms of initial cost or aggressiveness to the discs. Generally, the harder the brake pads the faster they will wear the discs, and sometimes the pads are so hard they

appear never to wear out; they just chew up the discs instead! They can also be extremely expensive, so it is possible that the cost of the pads relative to that of new discs will lead you to consider the discs as the sacrificial element in the braking system.

Hoses

Another worthwhile upgrade is replacing all flexible rubber brake hoses with braided steel hoses, usually referred to as 'aeroquip'. Like 'hoover', aeroquip is a brand name that has become a generic description – surely the ultimate accolade for any commercial product – and although there are now a number of alternatives, genuine Aeroquip is top-quality, and remains one of the leading brands.

Under extreme pressures, conventional rubber hoses may swell or expand slightly so the force applied at the pedal is not applied in full to the pads; there is some lost motion, felt as sponginess at the pedal. Steel-braided hoses will reduce expansion to an insignificant level, thereby improving brake response and feel. They are also far more resistant to damage, although this

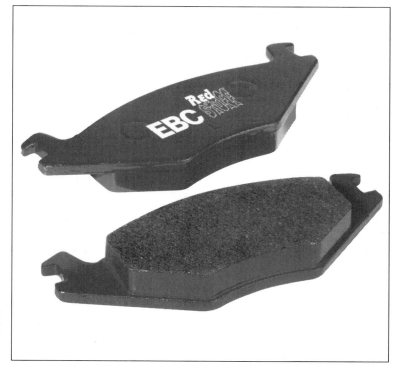

One of the easiest ways to improve braking performance on any vehicle is with high-performance brake pads. These will usually enhance braking performance with no discernible drawbacks.

may not be a major benefit unless you spend a lot of time in the 'rough'! Indeed, the reverse is more likely to be a problem as braided hose is incredibly aggressive when in contact with other components and can act like a coarse file, which in due course will abrade its way through most materials. Therefore you must be extremely careful when routing braided hoses; they must be free to move through the full range of suspension and steering movement, but prevented as far as practicable from contacting any other components, which is not always easy to achieve. Nevertheless, provided you can stop them chewing through your paintwork, or anything else that gets in their way, braided hoses are a worthwhile improvement and one of the few upgrades you can make with no discernible downside.

Knock-off

Another aspect of brake performance to be aware of is pad knock-off, which rarely if ever occurs on the road, but can in track use because of the kerbs and rumble strips used at many circuits. It feels a little like brake fade, but can happen very abruptly and unexpectedly. If you habitually make use of the rumble strips at speed the severe vibration induced can cause the disc to wobble, especially if there is even the slightest amount of play in the wheel bearings, although it can occur even when everything seems to be perfect. This appears to affect some cars more than others, which suggests a structural weakness somewhere, perhaps some flex in the hubs or suspension allowing the discs to run out of true in extreme situations.

This allows the disc to shimmy, which eases the pads back into the calipers (usually they run with a tiny clearance or even lightly brushing the disc, ready for the next application) so the next time you go for the middle pedal it goes to the floor because the stroke of the pedal is used just to take up the extra clearance. This is very disconcerting as it feels at first like complete brake failure. But if you are ready for it (or *very* quick-witted) and have allowed some margin for error in your

Conventional rubber hoses may swell or expand slightly when brakes are applied hard, reducing pressure applied to the pads. Steel-braided brake hoses, often referred to as aeroquip even though manufacturer Aeroquip is one of many, will help prevent this, and are a worthwhile addition to any braking system.

braking distance, you can come off the brake pedal and apply it again, which is usually enough to restore normality. Unfortunately, the usual reaction of most drivers when confronted with apparent brake failure is to press the pedal harder, which means all the braking effort goes on the rear brakes, and that virtually guarantees that they will lock up.

Anyone who has experienced this will vouch for the fact that locking up the rear wheels at high speed is not recommended! But assuming you have got away with it, you will probably learn to stay off the kerbs and rumble strips; alternatively you may prefer to give the brake pedal a light tap towards the end of the straights, just before you need to brake in earnest, which will take up the clearance caused by pad knock-off.

Reputations

As with so many other things in developing a car for track use, there is an element of trial-and-error in selecting the right pad material. Another complication is that you may be offered discs that allegedly are superior to the standard OE items, or that go together with a specific pad material to provide a superior combination. Many permutations may be available for the more popular vehicles and you need to evaluate the competing manufacturers' claims as best you can. However, I recommend that you stick to the more reputable brands and remember that quality must always be paid for; I would incline to be suspicious of anything that appeared to be too much of a bargain!

Assuming your car is a reasonably popular choice for track days, there may be a way of benefiting from other people's experience. Keep your eyes and ears open and ask the right questions, and you may discover a good combination for your car because others have already proven them; they will have done the testing and evaluation for you. While you may derive some satisfaction from discovering things for yourself, it can be a costly exercise, so don't be too proud to benefit from the experience of others. Other useful sources of information include owners' clubs and discussion forums on the Internet.

More cooling

A simple change of brake pad material can be enough to sort the braking problems on many cars, but if not the next step is to provide more cooling. Because of the effect of weight transfer under heavy braking, the front brakes do most of the work (probably as much as 80%, sometimes even more) on the average road-going car. For that reason it is unlikely that you will suffer from overheated rear brakes, so probably you will only need to cool the front brakes. The ideal is to direct cooling air to the hubs and rely on centrifugal force to allow it to radiate out through the vanes in the discs, which is the principle used in most high-tech racing cars. However, this feature is incorporated at the design stage, with specially designed hubs, uprights and brake rotors, and unless you have some very special design, engineering and fabrication skills at your disposal, it will be difficult to achieve anything similar with a modified road car. Usually the best we can achieve is to scoop in some high-pressure air from the vicinity of the front valance or spoiler and direct it via a length of flexible hose (central heating ducting tube usually) to the general vicinity of the disc. Because of the bulk of typical standard production suspension parts, space may be at a premium and you will need to route and secure the ducting carefully so that it doesn't interfere with suspension and steering movement. For that reason it may be easier to accommodate two lengths of small-bore hose, aimed at the front and rear of the disc, for example, rather than a single large-bore hose.

Bigger is better

If you have tried higher-spec brake pads and provided plenty of cooling air to the brakes, yet still suffer from overheating and fade, the next step is to change the hardware, to larger discs, calipers and so on. You may be lucky (or shrewd) enough to drive a vehicle for which a large number of performance 'goodies', including brake upgrades, are available. These may have been designed by the manufacturer for motorsport, or are parts from a larger or faster model from the same manufacturer's range, or they could be special aftermarket components. Again my advice would be to stick to reputable, well-known brands and be suspicious of anything that looks too much of a bargain.

Indeed, you may need to take a deep breath when obtaining quotes; brake hardware tends to be horrendously expensive, but because brakes are safety critical you cannot afford to cut corners. When you buy something that has been designed and developed for the application by a reputable manufacturer, at least you have some assurance that it will work as intended . . . or reasonable grounds for complaint if it doesn't.

Of the modifications you can make, one of the most effective and least likely to produce undesirable side effects is fitting larger-diameter discs, which are beneficial as they provide greater leverage. To visualize this, think about a slowly spinning cycle wheel and how easy it is to stop it spinning by snagging one of the spokes near the rim; then envisage how much more difficult the wheel is to stop when you try to grab a spoke near the hub. Larger discs may also provide marginally more cooling because of their greater surface area. If they are available for your vehicle, therefore, they will be well worth considering as there are several benefits with no real downside apart perhaps from a modest increase in unsprung weight. Assuming the bigger discs will work with the existing calipers, they can be fitted with no other modifications to the braking system and should not affect the brake balance significantly provided the increase in diameter (which will usually be dictated by what will fit within the existing wheel) is modest.

If you drive a less common vehicle for which performance parts are not readily available, however, you will have to make some difficult decisions. You need considerable skill and expertise to modify the brake system effectively, and there are many pitfalls to beware of; this is definitely an area where a little knowledge can be dangerous.

By changing the size of the discs and calipers you will be altering the brake system's mechanical and hydraulic force ratios, and probably the swept area of the friction surfaces as well, all of which have been carefully calculated by the vehicle manufacturer to give the right brake balance front to rear, with a reasonable pedal stroke and effort. You may be able to improve the brake system, but it is also possible to inadvertently make it worse with inexpert modifications. If you fit new discs and/or calipers, among other factors you need to ensure that the calipers are soundly mounted and perfectly aligned with the discs, both laterally and radially. If you get it wrong you may end up with brakes that are either ludicrously easy to lock up or impossible to lock, or with poor balance causing them to lock prematurely at one end or the other, or with either a soft pedal with long travel or a hard pedal requiring superhuman strength to get maximum braking. Most problems of this nature can be solved with sufficient time, money and know-how, but unless you have a full and thorough understanding of brake system design, you had best leave well alone, or seek expert professional advice.

As I have already pointed out, brake hardware tends to be expensive anyway, and if you are paying for professional expertise to redesign your braking system (which is effectively what you will be doing), the cost is likely to be prohibitive and you need to decide whether it is justifiable. If you are seriously hampered by poor braking performance, though, it may behove you to consider a more suitable vehicle for track days, unless you have a particular attachment to it, in which case you may have to learn to brake more gently and just live with its shortcomings . . . or buy a Porsche.

6

SUSPENSION DEVELOPMENT

If you take to the track for the first time in a standard production car, it is almost a certainty that the handling will be disappointing. If you are new to track days, then initially you should concentrate on improving your driving, as there are probably more performance gains to be found in the driver than in the car. After a time, however, your driving will undoubtedly improve, and with a few track miles under your tyres you will also have the experience to identify ways in which the car could be improved to match your new-found skills.

Influence

In *Tyre Care* I stressed the importance of static suspension geometry in obtaining the best possible performance from the tyres. Once you have the suspension geometry somewhere near right you can think about spring and damper rates. Or alternatively, once you are satisfied that you have the spring and damper rates in the ballpark you can start to optimize your geometry. This merely highlights the essential problem of suspension development; namely that every aspect of suspension operation has an influence on, and is in turn influenced by, everything else. Therefore every modification you make will affect something else, and probably several things. You need to remember that your sole contact with *terra firma* is the footprint of your four tyres, each no larger than the palm of your hand. At the same time, because driving is an interactive business – as well as giving driving commands, we also need to react to what the car does – all of the messages and sensations you get back from the car are transmitted via the tyres. Every modification you make to the car, therefore, should be aimed at optimizing the performance of those four tiny patches of rubber.

Dilemma

The eternal dilemma in handling is that in order to achieve maximum roadholding the tyres need to be in contact with the ground as much as possible and with as even a contact pressure as practicable, and in order to achieve this you need soft springs to allow the wheels to follow the contours of the road. However, under the influence of centrifugal force (centripetal for the pedants out there!), during hard cornering the body rolls, which is both uncomfortable for the driver and any passengers and may also play havoc with suspension geometry such that the wheels are no longer held perpendicular, with the tread square to the road surface. And in order to control body roll you need firm springs, the exact opposite to what you need to conform to surface irregularities.

If you like, in one mode the wheels are moving relative to the body; and in the other the body is moving relative to the wheels. To control movement of the wheels

The powerful legs of a highly trained downhill ski racer are the most sophisticated 'active' suspension system known, all controlled by that enormously powerful computer, the human brain. This is Formula One driver Jacques Villeneuve in action during a winter break.

relative to the body you require soft springs; but to control movement of the body relative to the wheels you need firm springs. Of course, in the real world it is not even as simple as that. The car is liable to hit a bump or two during hard cornering so you cannot divorce the two functions, even if it were mechanically possible to do so; the only way would be with electronics and active suspension.

The most sophisticated suspension system known to man is the human leg. Take the case of the downhill ski racer who uses an enormous amount of muscular

strength to resist cornering forces in a high-speed turn, yet is still able to react instantly and accurately to the most minute changes in the terrain in order to maintain an even keel. His muscles function as springs and dampers in one, but that is only possible because he has an enormously powerful and sophisticated computer . . . his brain . . . making the necessary calculations of force and resistance with great speed and precision. Incredible . . .

Although the primary purpose of active suspension in Formula One was to ensure a

Active suspension in Formula One, as in the Williams-Renault FW14 that took British hero Nigel Mansell to the World Championship in 1992, was designed not to offer the driver a smoother ride, but to ensure that the all-important wings were maintained at the optimum angle at all times.

stable aerodynamic platform and not necessarily to resolve the above conflict, it is a shame that this avenue of development was closed off as it might in due course have produced real benefits to road car users. So how do we resolve the conflicting needs for both soft springs (over the bumps) and hard springs (in the bends)? Yet again, we *compromise*.

Trial and error

Spring rates are always a compromise, and the rates arrived at by most manufacturers are extremely conservative, with a decided bias towards ride comfort over handling. Rightly so, as most customers are more interested in a comfortable ride than in ultimate handling and roadholding. It is my experience that spring rates on the average road car can be increased by 50-100% without *serious* deterioration in ride quality, although obviously there will be some trade-off. Although it is impossible to quantify, you may be able to achieve, say, a 20% improvement in handling and roadholding for a 10% deterioration in ride quality. Despite the many advances in car design over recent years, and the use of computers to design or calculate just about everything, the time-honoured way of calculating spring rates is still trial-and-error. Fortunately, conventional coil springs are relatively inexpensive, so trying-and-erring needn't break the bank.

Show business

As a rule, the stickier the tyres fitted to your car the stiffer springs you will need as the more 'g' force you generate the more the car will roll. If you are considering changing suspension springs you can also consider lowering the car, which is one of the easiest and most beneficial things you can do to improve cornering speed and performance.

Many cars, especially the sportier models, look fantastic when they are announced under the glare of the spotlights at some glitzy motor show launch. Yet when you see them on the road some months later, somehow they don't look quite as sharp. That is because the manufacturers' marketing people know the value of a slinky ride height in making the car appear more attractive. Back in the real world, though, when the car is released for sale it will usually ride several inches higher as the manufacturers build in a huge margin to allow for the heaviest loads, highest speeds and roughest roads likely to be encountered, such that no part of the body or suspension can ever contact the ground, and the tyres can never so much as kiss the wheelarches under any combination of steering lock and suspension deflection. The manufacturers dread warranty claims arising from their vehicles bottoming out or catching tyres on wheelarches, and they are even more fearful of liability claims (consider the possibility of a tyre failure caused by prolonged or repeated contact with, say, a wheelarch lip) that may arise from the same causes.

Most cars therefore can be lowered substantially, especially when you can be certain the car will not be driven heavily laden, or on rough roads. The difference is not just cosmetic. Lowering a car is highly beneficial as it lowers the centre of gravity and reduces weight transfer. As we shall see later, it is the amount of weight transferred in cornering that ultimately dictates the amount of cornering force the car can develop, and hence limits our speed on any given corner, so anything we can do to reduce the weight transfer will allow faster cornering. The mechanical factors that influence weight transfer (ignoring for the moment the dynamic factors of corner radius and speed) are vehicle weight, track width and centre of gravity height. Therefore anything we can do to reduce weight, increase track width, or lower the C of G will improve cornering force and hence speed.

Pitfalls

Beware, however, of lowering a car too much. There are two serious pitfalls, quite apart from the obvious ones of bottoming out and scraping bits on the road or catching tyres on the wheelarches. One is that – depending on the suspension layout and geometry – you can disturb the carefully designed-in relationship between the roll centre and the centre of gravity; or more accurately the mass centroid axis. There is not the space here for a complicated explanation of these largely theoretical concepts, which are primarily of interest to suspension designers; suffice to say that this can create all sorts of complications.

For example, you might lower the roll centre by more than you lower the centre of gravity, ie you could lower the car and with it the mass centroid axis by, say, 50mm, but in doing so drop the roll centre by 75 or 100mm, perhaps even more, because of some quirk in the geometry (this is especially true of the MacPherson Strut, one of the most popular suspension designs in existence). Therefore, because the roll centre and mass centroid axis have moved further apart, the car will tend to roll more, not less, because of the extra leverage exerted. This will tend to play havoc with the suspension geometry and possibly prevent the tyre tread from sitting squarely on the road.

The opposite can also happen, although this is less likely. However, if the mass centroid axis moves closer to the roll centre the car will roll less. You might suppose this to be a good thing, but in fact it will probably cause the vehicle to lift one or both inside wheels instead; if taken too far it can even cause the car to tip over altogether . . . clearly an undesirable state of affairs. (For evidence of this phenomenon, look at a few videos featuring SuperTouring car racing and ask yourself why some cars appear to ride the kerbs beautifully and others are thrown violently up on two wheels by contact with the kerbs.)

The other danger of excessive lowering is that you use up most of the available bump travel unless you go to the trouble of revising the suspension location points, swapping the dampers for ones with a shorter stroke, etc. Most cars seem to be designed with around 60% of the damper stroke available for bump travel and 40% for droop. If you lower the car using the existing dampers and suspension geometry, you may change that ratio to 40% bump and 60% droop, or even 30:70%. That leaves very little stroke available for bump, and even at static ride height you

may be perilously close to riding on the bump stops; once you are rolling in the corners it doesn't take much of a bump to use up the remaining available damper stroke and ride on the bump stops. This is a bad thing as the suspension effectively goes solid momentarily and the tyre becomes overloaded, causing instant loss of grip and possibly loss of control. The sensation you will feel from the driving seat is of a tyre that grips and lets go, grips and lets go, faster than you can read about it, in a highly unpredictable and disconcerting manner. If this happens in a high-speed curve you have to be highly skilled – or lucky! – to maintain control.

You can reduce this problem by fitting stiffer springs – so the suspension does not compress as easily – and progressive microcellular bump stops, but the essential problem is lack of available wheel travel, so there are no easy answers. Whatever you do, don't think you can solve the problem simply by cutting short the bump stops, or even removing them altogether, to give you more travel. You will still have the same problem, only you will also destroy the

Although many people refer to them as shock absorbers, dampers do not absorb shocks: the springs do. Dampers are incorporated into the suspension system in order to damp the action of the spring.

internal workings of the dampers (which the bump stops are there to protect) in no time.

The real solution is not to lower the car too much, or if you really must, to make sure the suspension geometry and damper lengths are revised accordingly. Realistically that sort of modification is probably beyond the scope of the keen amateur as you really need to know what you are doing (and sometimes I wonder if even the pros *really* know what they're doing!). You require enough theoretical knowledge to understand suspension geometry and redesign accordingly, and you need the practical knowledge to be able to design and manufacture suspension components. Bearing in mind that your life may depend on it, this is not a field for dabbling in!

Damping

Depending on how much you lower and/or stiffen the springs, you may need different dampers, or shock absorbers as some people prefer to call them. The term shock absorber is a misnomer and leads to many misconceptions as to the nature and purpose of dampers and their interaction with the springs. In reality the springs absorb the shocks and dampers exist to dampen the action of the springs.

Without some form of damping, a spring when compressed and released will continue to compress and rebound, compress and rebound – boing, boing, boing! – until it runs out of energy which, as the only resistance is the internal friction generated by the molecules rubbing against one another, may take some time. In order to control this motion dampers provide more friction and turn this energy into heat. If you want to see the effect of bad (or non-existent) damping look at a kid on a pogo stick, and if you want to see the effect of good damping look at some of the latest WRC rally cars and marvel at how they fly off a crest or brow, soak up the impact on landing and return immediately to their normal ride height with no secondary bounce . . . unbelievable.

It should be apparent that damping is closely related to spring rate, although sadly there does not seem to be any way of relating these two directly . . . not in the public domain anyway. If any of the damper manufacturers or leading race or rally teams have a method of calculating the damping required for a specific spring or wheel rate they are keeping it to themselves! Once again trial-and-error seems to be the favoured method of arriving at the desired damping rates.

The function of the damper, therefore, is to return the wheel as quickly as possible to its 'normal' position (*ie* ride height, usually) when the spring has been deflected by some irregularity in the road surface, by damping the uncontrolled motion of the spring. The dampers will also have a considerable influence on the way in which the car rolls in cornering, but contrary to popular belief they have no influence on *how much* the car rolls; only on how quickly. This defines how rapidly the car will take a 'set' when it has been turned into a corner.

Like spring rates, damping rates are a compromise. You may, for example, prefer the dampers to be stiff in bump, so the car takes a set relatively slowly and in a smoothly controlled manner when you turn into a corner. However, this may make the car harsh and unforgiving over the bumps, so you need to trade off a little of one for the other. This is where adjustable dampers come into their own. In my experience, the damping – especially bump damping – has a greater influence on ride quality than spring rates. With adjustable dampers you can stiffen them up for the track to improve roll control, trading off a bit of ride comfort. Most race tracks nowadays are pretty smooth, so achieving good compliance over the bumps is not a big issue, but achieving good control of body roll may be. On the road you will be cornering more slowly (hopefully!) and the surface will be bumpier, so you can adjust the dampers to a softer setting for the drive home.

Confusion

Multi-adjustable dampers are a means for achieving the best of both worlds by utilizing separate controls for high-speed and low-speed damping. When the body rolls as you turn into a corner the suspension compresses relatively slowly, at least compared to when you hit a bump or ridge in the road at speed. Therefore the low-speed damping can be made fairly stiff for good control of body roll and the high-speed damping can be fairly soft for good compliance over bumps. When you add in controls for both low- and high-speed rebound adjustment, though, there is plenty of scope for confusion.

Until you have considerable track day driving experience (and even when you have) it can be very difficult to feel what the dampers are doing and decide what you want them to do. If you are using a popular car for track days it may be worth seeking advice from other owners, and if there is some sort of consensus as to a good set-up, simply emulate that. Bear in mind that for track days you should be striving primarily to make your car predictable and enjoyable to drive, and not, perhaps, striving for the last word in performance.

Paper clips

Anti-roll bars are an effective means of controlling body roll and fine-tuning handling, although they have a couple of disadvantages. To some extent they inhibit the independence of the suspension, although this needn't be regarded as much of a handicap unless you are using a really hefty bar. They also act as a spring which is effectively undamped, although obviously the dampers will also have some effect on the bar. The size of the anti-roll bar should be appropriate to the rate of the springs; if you have fitted very heavy-duty springs in an endeavour to control body roll it may be preferable to use a heavier anti-roll bar in conjunction with slightly softer springs, or conversely, if you are using a really heavy anti-roll bar an increase in spring rates may be called for, always bearing in mind that an effective anti-roll bar is a much more efficient means of reducing or controlling body roll than massive springs. So you see the choice of anti-roll bar influences the choice of springs, and *vice versa*.

It shouldn't be difficult to improve on the anti-roll bar fitted to the average production saloon or sports car. Most are very flimsy, many are made of poor-quality materials and some are poorly designed; no better than 'bent paper clips', as some might say. Almost invariably any compromises are forced on the designers by packaging considerations, although cost is

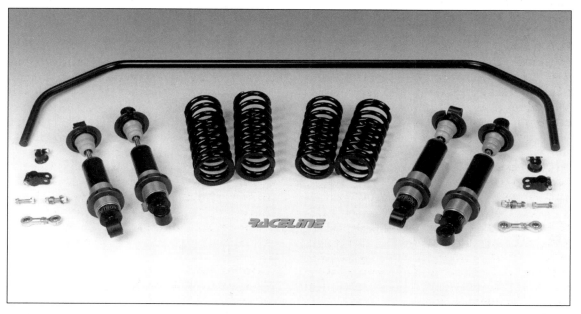

An anti-roll bar is much more effective in controlling body roll than uprated suspension springs, but must be well designed in order to work as intended. This is Raceline's 'bar for the Lotus Elise.

also a major factor in production engineering.

Packaging an anti-roll bar effectively is not easy, but ideally the working portion of the bar should be as straight as possible; the mounting points on the suspension should be as far outboard as possible; the pivots on the chassis should be as far apart as possible; the arms should be as short as possible; and the drop links should be reasonably long, especially if the bar is adjustable. This ensures that the bar works as it should, by twisting rather than bending, that it exerts the maximum possible leverage and there are no problems with articulation of the drop links. In practice it may be possible to achieve some of these objectives, but not all of them, and some compromises are almost inevitable.

A decent range of adjustment allows you to fine-tune the handling. In *Vehicle Dynamics*, we will examine more fully how the amount of weight transferred in cornering is what ultimately determines the amount of cornering force the car can develop, and hence limits our speed on any given corner. However, it is rare for a car to be exactly neutral in cornering; usually the tyre slip angle at one end of the car will be slightly higher than at the other. There may be a number of reasons for this, but one of the most influential factors is that the weight transferred may not be evenly distributed between front and rear. The ratio of weight transferred at the front, relative to the total weight transfer, is known as the roll couple distribution. By adjusting the anti-roll bars, we alter the roll couple distribution.

The guiding principle to remember is that increasing the roll stiffness at one end of the car will increase weight transfer at that end, which in turn will increase the tyre slip angle at that end. We can utilize this knowledge to seek a more neutral handling balance. Bear in mind, though, that adjusting the anti-roll bar will not affect the *total* amount of weight transferred, as what is gained at one end will be lost at the other, so it doesn't require a huge change in anti-roll bar adjustment to achieve a considerable change in roll couple distribution. The anti-roll bar is therefore quite sensitive to adjustment and should be treated accordingly.

A few cars have both front and rear anti-roll bars, but most make do with just a front bar. As a rule, stiffening the front bar will result in increased understeer (because more weight will be transferred to the outside front tyre, causing it to assume a greater slip angle) and softening it will reduce understeer, but the rule is not incontrovertible so your first few laps after any adjustment should be approached with caution.

Brace yourself

Although not strictly part of the suspension, another worthwhile modification is the strut brace. The majority of modern cars use MacPherson Strut front suspension, largely because it is simple, reasonably effective and, most compelling of all for the motor manufacturers, cheap to produce. Therefore, most cars have suspension mountings, commonly referred to as strut towers, high within the engine bay to locate the top mount of the strut. Because of the space taken up by the engine and transmission, the engine bay inevitably represents a large open space in the bodyshell, which is prone to flex and distortion under extreme conditions. A strut brace is a sturdy metal brace that is fitted over the engine and mounted to the top of the strut towers, and serves to prevent them from flexing inwards. This helps to maintain the structural integrity of the bodyshell in hard use, which in turn ensures that the suspension works as designed.

Location

Another aspect of suspension development to consider is location. To minimize NVH (motor industry shorthand for noise, vibration and harshness) most manufacturers use rubber bushes in the suspension mountings to isolate the chassis from the road as much as practicable. They also offer the further benefit of taking up production tolerances, allowing manufacturers a little leeway in the

Suspension bushes made of polyurethane, like these Powerflex bushes for the Lotus Elise, offer far more positive location than conventional rubber-and-metal bushes, allowing the suspension to move in the manner intended by the designer, yet without any of the disadvantages of spherical bearings, like excessive noise and harshness.

Greater cornering speeds encountered on the circuit may lead to oil surge problems, unless the sump is expertly baffled. This is Raceline's Performance Engineered sump for the Ford Zetec engine, intended for in-line installation in the Caterham Seven and other specialist sports cars.

location of suspension pickup points, although with modern Computer Aided Design (the CAD in CAD/CAM) techniques, bodyshells are nowadays manufactured much more accurately than they once were. Nevertheless, the use of rubber bushes persists. Unfortunately, these rubber bushes, while they undoubtedly have the desired effect, also allow a lot of unwanted deflection, so the suspension geometry departs from the designed ideal under heavy cornering or braking loads. The forces generated are considerable, but the amount of deflection is nevertheless surprising. Under heavy braking, for example, the designed-in castor (typically

3-8deg positive) can disappear to zero, or even go negative in extreme cases. Powerflex urethane suspension bushes are now available for a large number of vehicles and offer much more positive suspension location for very little if any increase in transmitted NVH. The result is much more precise handling . . . a worthwhile trade-off in my view.

If you lower and/or stiffen the suspension you may find the geometry is no longer appropriate. The car will roll less (theoretically anyway), so you may be able to reduce static camber angles as the amount of camber change in roll will be reduced. As I have said before, every change you make will affect something else, and probably several things. This has a knock-on effect, and sometimes you may feel that for every two steps forward you are taking one step back! It may be time-consuming and sometimes frustrating, but nevertheless it is important to proceed as logically and methodically as possible.

You should also bear in mind that increasing the cornering potential of your car may have other undesirable effects. If the sump is not adequately baffled, for example, you may get oil surge, leading to oil draining away from the pickup under the influence of centrifugal force in cornering. Wide pressure fluctuation in the corners is a sure sign of oil surge, which means the bearings are being starved of oil as the pump is sucking air; any sort of oil surge or pressure fluctuation demands immediate investigation and rectification. You might get away with a momentary occurrence as the oil film clinging to the metal surfaces offers some protection, but if it is in any way prolonged or repeated it is guaranteed to spell disaster for your engine: note, not suspected or potential, but *guaranteed*.

Lowest priority

If you are faced with rebuilding your engine after meeting disaster on the track you may be tempted to look for more power. You will note, however, that I have not mentioned engine tuning at all until now, and there are several reasons for this. One is that many books are available which cover this highly technical subject more thoroughly and expertly than I could hope to. The second is that as engines have become more complex and sophisticated the scope for amateur tuners has become limited; the majority of enthusiasts now prefer to leave engine tuning to professional engine builders, with good reason because they have the necessary skills, knowledge, experience, facilities, equipment and components. Lastly, but perhaps most important of all, engine power should be virtually the lowest of your priorities. When you embark on track days, by far the greatest performance gains will come from learning to drive the car to its full potential. When you are confident you are getting everything out of it that's already there, you can try to improve the handling, roadholding and perhaps braking, as these will yield far greater gains than more horsepower. Only after all this has been accomplished should you consider looking for more power.

Summary

Before you set off for your first track day, you must ensure that your car is mechanically sound. You don't need a specially prepared car for track days, but you should at least do some basic mechanical checks to ensure the car is sound and safe to use on the circuit. As a minimum, you should check all fluid levels; check brake pad thickness; ensure that the wheel nuts are torqued to the correct setting; adjust tyre pressures; and carry out a very thorough visual examination of the tyres for wear or damage. Ideally most of these checks should be completed before you leave home, preferably several days before your track day, giving you time to rectify any problems. Try to avoid using brand new 'sticker' tyres if you can, but equally bear in mind that you will need sufficient tyre tread depth to get home again at the end of the day. The same goes for brake pads. When you arrive, and depending on how far you have had to drive to the circuit, you may wish to dip the oil and do a final check of tyre pressure before you go on track. Then you will be ready to start driving.

7

DRIVING APPROACH

Like most car enthusiasts, you probably think you're a good driver. You drive pretty fast, right? You have been known to hang the tail out a bit when accelerating away from a T-junction. You squeal the tyres when negotiating the odd roundabout. And you often get a squeal from the back seat when you're taking your mother-in-law to the shops! Maybe you've even had a trial or introductory lesson with one of the racing schools at one of the famous motor racing circuits scattered around the country, or done a track day at one of those circuits, so you already know the ropes. Yup . . . you're pretty handy behind the wheel all right.

If that applies to you then track days should be right up your street, but unless you have had considerable circuit driving experience already, you may be in for a bit of a surprise. The fact is that driving fast on a race circuit is *totally* different to driving fast on the road, as we have already said. One thing is certain: it's not as easy as it looks on the telly! You may think you're pretty quick, but to drive on the road anywhere near as fast as you can on a closed race circuit would be criminally irresponsible. That is why, if you *really* want to drive fast, you should try and do it on a closed circuit, where speed is not just tolerated: it's encouraged.

On a race circuit you don't have to worry about staying on your side of the road; traffic coming in the opposite direction (well not usually, anyway!); speed

limits; speed cameras; sleeping policemen; slightly dozy policemen; big blokes in uniform pointing hairdryers at you; massive artics; caravans; Volvos; old blokes in trilby hats driving rusty Metros; cyclists; pedestrians; stop signs; traffic lights; and all the other hazards of the open road. There's just you and that endless ribbon of tarmac, inviting you to go as fast as you can.

Safety first

That's not to say that anything goes, mind you. You have a duty to yourself and to other track users to drive safely and responsibly, while always bearing in mind that no matter how much care is taken, things may still go wrong. Speed is dangerous, and a fast car can injure, maim or kill. But we humans are fascinated by danger, and maybe that's part of the attraction and why motor sport has always had such attraction to competitors and spectators alike.

But as I intimated in my *Introduction*, the powers-that-be in motor racing seem still to be overwhelmed by the Imola 1994 tragedy and its worldwide exposure on television. Certainly, with the possible exception of the assassination of US president John F Kennedy (an event repeated endlessly since, but one which wasn't witnessed 'live' by many), there has never been a more public death than that of Ayrton Senna.

There is a huge difference between driving fast on the road and driving fast on the circuit, where you can use all of the road to maintain cornering speeds.

So understandably perhaps, there is nowadays a desire to make motor racing completely safe, not just for the spectators and officials, but also for the drivers, which you could argue is either impossible, or only possible if you ruin its essential character. Motor racing has a primary duty to protect the paying spectators, because they have paid good money to see a spectacle in the reasonable expectation that they won't come to any harm. Then it has a secondary duty to protect volunteer marshals and others involved in the organization of any event, although because their duties give them privileged access to 'the inner sanctum' they have to be prepared to accept a higher level of risk; marshals, for example, get closer to the action than any spectator, but that inevitably and quite reasonably carries that higher level of risk. Finally, it has a duty to protect competitors from any unnecessary, obvious and foreseeable hazards. What it cannot do is protect competitors from *all* risk, as it seems to be striving to do at present.

In the cause of safety, spectators are moved further and further away from the trackside, reducing the spectacle, while the circuits are being made more and more homogeneous, so reducing the challenge. Most Formula One circuits nowadays consist largely of slow to medium-speed corners and chicanes linked by fairly short straights (because this is necessarily a generalization there are many obvious exceptions, but the general point is nonetheless valid). Some great circuits and some great corners are being lost as a result. The supreme irony, of course, is that many of the drivers mourn the loss of these challenges. If this trend continues unchecked, motor racing won't be worth watching . . . and it certainly won't be worth doing! There has got to be some danger, or else there is no challenge. If anyone could stroll to the summit of Mount Everest, would anyone bother? You need to have a healthy respect for the danger but not remove it entirely.

Whatever safety measures are put in

place, human beings, being the sad and silly creatures we are, will usually squander them by taking greater risks. Years ago, before seat belts became compulsory in race cars and drivers were routinely flung out of overturning cars, they would never have *dreamed* of banging wheels with another competitor in defence of a position. Nowadays it is an accepted practice; indeed you are considered a wuss if you don't, which happened to Damon Hill when he questioned the tactics and track ethics of some of his Formula One contemporaries. No genuine motorsport enthusiast wants to see anyone get hurt, but let's face it, if motor racing were to be guaranteed 100% safe it wouldn't have the same appeal. The only way to guarantee the safety of all competitors in motor sports is to stop it, which none of us wants. The same is true of track days. You can never make them completely safe: what you need to do is make them *acceptably* safe.

Responsibilities to others

Therefore you must always bear in mind your responsibilities to the other track users. Careless, irresponsible or over-aggressive driving will not be tolerated by most organizers, and will definitely be frowned upon by your fellow track users. Everyone accepts that when you are pushing the limits, mistakes are inevitable. Thankfully, most are fairly harmless. But you should never forget that mistakes *can* be costly. The closer you get to the edge the easier it becomes to make a mistake, which is all well and good except that on a track day there is a good chance you may involve someone else. Damaging your own car is a matter between you and your bank manager; but causing or contributing to damage to a fellow track user's treasured motor is rightly regarded as unacceptable. And there is also the element of danger to consider: people could be injured – or worse – as a result of your recklessness, bravado

One of the great attractions of track days is the camaraderie that exists between drivers, all of whom, despite their allegiance to different marques, are motor enthusiasts to the core. Don't spoil it by selfish or thoughtless actions.

On any track day you will encounter drivers with a broad range of abilities and motivations, and vehicles with very different performance capabilities. In the normal scheme of things some will be slower and some will be faster than you, and you must always be prepared to make allowances for other track users.

or lack of judgment. Even plunging into the gravel trap all by yourself, which on the face of it harms nobody, still has repercussions. It will likely cause the session to be stopped and the track to be closed while the stranded vehicle is recovered, resulting in loss of precious track time to all other track users.

Most track day enthusiasts, because they are also pushing the envelope and have themselves probably made the occasional mistake, are reasonably tolerant of others' mistakes. Go off once causing the session to be stopped and you are probably in for a bit of a ribbing; but do it too often and you will quickly make yourself unpopular. As the *camaraderie* of getting together with a group of like-minded motor enthusiasts is one of the fundamental pleasures of track days, it is probably as well to avoid making a pariah of yourself!

Benefits

However, learning to drive fast in the relative safety of a race circuit can have enormous benefits. When we first learn to drive a car we don't really learn to drive at all; we merely learn how to pass the statutory driving test. The real lessons start when we take to the road. If daily driving is the School of Hard Knox, then high-speed circuit driving might be regarded as the University. First of all it will teach you what your car is really capable of. Many ordinary motorists have *no idea* . . . It may also teach you what *you* are capable of, or not, as the case may be! Whilst I would not wish this on anyone, having a mishap on the track can also teach you a pretty healthy respect for how quickly and easily things can go wrong, and the possible consequences.

Either way, these are valuable lessons, which will doubtless stand you in good stead in subsequent road driving. Perhaps even more beneficially, getting your fill of driving fast on track days may help to get it out of your system, so that there is little temptation to risk life, limbs and licence once you're back on the open road. But above all, driving fast is fun!

Making allowances

Although they are all there ostensibly to have fun and enjoy themselves, people attending track days have very different approaches and motivations. Some drivers who own a fast car may use the track day just to give the car a good workout, something that is not often possible in today's traffic conditions (and even if it were, it is doubtful whether the social climate allows it). These guys may push their cars pretty hard, but are not too bothered about pushing themselves. They are the ones that stand around talking about their cars between sessions.

Others view a track day as a form of advanced driver training and are anxious to learn all they can about fast driving. Some of them are apparently on a mission to push themselves to the limit at every turn. They may even have aspirations to race in due course. These guys can usually be found between sessions in earnest discussion with like-minded individuals about lines, braking and other elements of driving technique.

At most track days you will find a smattering of drivers who have had some competition experience. Sometimes they will be active drivers doing a little instructing to help finance their racing, or getting in a little bit of sly circuit familiarization in preparation for a forthcoming event.

Then there are those who profess to prefer doing track days, often claiming that they "can't afford to go motor racing any more". That may be a moot point. The average club race may give you 10-15 minutes practice – long enough for 10 laps, perhaps – to go with a 10-lap race. So at a club meeting you'll be lucky to do 50 miles, and frequently much less. On a track day, however, provided the track is 'open' (ie not restricted to sessions) and there are not too many stoppages, you can soon clock up a lot of miles; 200 miles or more in a day is not uncommon. That of course is also one of the attractions of track days – that you get much more track time – but it does lead to a good deal more wear and tear on the car and hence expense. Certainly the sums some people are prepared to expend on doing track days in a year, say, would easily finance a season of racing in one of the cheaper categories.

Regardless of the economics, some of these current or ex-racing drivers can be a menace, especially those who, because of their experience or track record (or egos!), regard themselves as above any rules the organizers may have made. Often they seem to consider track days as competitive events, and they use the experience they have gained in competition to terrorize and intimidate other track users with needlessly aggressive driving. Indeed, we sometimes suspect their motives; perhaps they find it easier to 'win' on a track day than in a real race! Sadly, it seems there is little that can be done to control their attitudes and behaviour, as in most cases they do at least know what they are doing. No one questions their competence: it is their effect on other track users – for which they apparently feel no responsibility – which causes concern. They are usually the ones standing around talking about themselves between sessions!

The lesson to be learnt from this is that at any track day you will find people with a wide range of attitudes and abilities, and you must be prepared to make allowances for others, whichever end of the spectrum you belong. If you find you are being held up by some fumbling novice who is apparently unable or unwilling to look in his mirrors . . . chill out. Or, if you feel you are the victim of some unnecessarily aggressive overtaking . . . chill out! You are there to enjoy yourself, and so is everyone else, so there is no point in allowing yourself to get stressed out about the actions of others, over which you have no control. Above all, you should concentrate on what *you* are doing, and not allow yourself to become distracted by what others are doing.

Eliminating the competition
You should never lose sight of the fact that track days are strictly non-competitive events. The organizers have usually 'sold' them to the circuit owner and, more importantly, their insurers on that basis. If you are tempted to think otherwise, look around you. There are no cheering fans in the grandstands; there is nobody to wave a chequered flag at you; no trophy to be waved triumphantly aloft; no national

anthem playing (praise be!); no trophy girl to be kissed; no prize money to be won; no glory to be gained.

This means there should be no racing, so if you find that the thrill of dicing with other cars is what really moves you, or if you find you get a real buzz out of overtaking others, then maybe you should consider taking the ARDS (Association of Racing Drivers Schools) course, obtaining a competition licence, and going racing, as actual competition may be a more suitable outlet for your competitive tendencies. At least then going to the ragged edge actually means something worthwhile, whereas if you drive aggressively and delight in carving people up just for the hell of it on a track day, you simply end up looking like a prat.

The non-competitive nature of track days also means that any form of lap timing is strictly prohibited. No one can pretend that no timing ever takes place on a track day, but strictly speaking it would probably invalidate any public liability insurance in place if exposed. Therefore if you are taking times or someone is doing it for you, do the organizers a favour and be discreet. Although some take a very firm stance, most organizers are prepared to turn a blind eye so long as stopwatches are not waved under their noses. In the event of a serious incident they need to be able to tell their insurers, with a clear conscience, that they were not *aware* of any timing taking place; and if they haven't seen it they are not aware of it, right? Don't make it unnecessarily difficult for them.

Incidentally, if there is a serious accident on track, then *anyone* who has been timing cars should take immediate steps to hide the evidence, even if they have no connection with the driver(s) involved. Zero the stopwatch, or switch it off altogether, and discreetly put it away; and if you have some times recorded and want

Grand Prix winners get to spray champagne over their adoring fans, a 'pleasure' that is denied track day drivers. Seriously, you should never forget that track days are supposed to be non-competitive.

to keep them for posterity, put them somewhere safe where they won't readily be found. The insurers, as is their wont, will do anything they can to avoid a claim, and if they were to discover someone with times written down, or with a stopwatch running, say, this could seriously jeopardize any claim. Although it is unlikely that they would have an investigator on the spot immediately, you never know who might be lurking about, and if they did by some chance discover evidence that someone was timing cars it might be just the excuse they were looking for.

However, let us not be unduly pessimistic, and dwell on what may go wrong. After all, the purpose of this guide is largely to encourage you to have a go. If you approach track days with the right attitude there should be no reason for anything to go wrong. Granted, the unexpected can always happen, but the means to minimize any risk is largely in your own hands.

Mental preparation

Let us assume that you want to get the best from yourself and your machine, but without unnecessary risk. You must be prepared to apply yourself and really concentrate. Although you don't have to treat it like the world championship, nevertheless it clearly behoves you to approach the task with some seriousness of purpose and a willingness to learn. Whatever you can do to familiarize yourself with the circuit beforehand is useful, whether reading the *Autosport* Circuit Guide, watching in-car videos or playing computer games, all of which can be surprisingly useful and at least shorten your learning curve a little. They will not help you acquire a feel for the car, however, and just because you have watched *In-Car 956* at the Nürburgring a hundred times, it

doesn't mean you don't have to treat the circuit with enormous respect when you are actually driving there for the first time! Many track day organizers offer optional instruction, which may prove useful; and if you are learning a new circuit and the organizers offer a novices' session, it would obviously behove you to avail yourself of it.

If you are prepared to approach track days in this way you should find you are amply rewarded. Track days offer you the opportunity to test your car in a way that wouldn't be possible on the open road and to develop an awareness of its capabilities – and limitations! – in a controlled environment. You get to drive on some of the world's most famous and evocative motor racing circuits, following in the wheel tracks of some of the legends of motorsports. They also offer the chance to test yourself. I believe that most drivers can benefit from the experience of driving at high speed, and that the skills and confidence that they acquire in the process will enhance their road driving and safety awareness. You get the chance to mingle with and enjoy the company of a group of car nuts, most of whom will have similar interests to your own, and to benefit from the shared experience. There may be much to be learnt from riding with other, more accomplished drivers. You may make new friends. You also get to admire some tasty motors . . .

Safety is, or should be, of paramount importance. You should always be aware that driving fast is intrinsically hazardous; it can never be made entirely safe. But it is also fun, and having fun whilst maintaining an acceptable level of safety is what you should aim for. Before you set off on your first track day, however, it will be helpful to understand a little about how your car works. And that is the subject of *Vehicle Dynamics*.

8

VEHICLE DYNAMICS

Your own driving experience will tell you that you can take a long sweeping corner faster than you can a tight hairpin. This is because the tyres have a finite amount of grip, or cornering force: that is, they will allow the car to generate a fixed amount of lateral acceleration, commonly expressed in units of gravity, or 'g'. If this were not the case we could take any corner at maximum speed, which clearly is not the case.

Inertia

Even those with only a rudimentary knowledge of physics will know that a body in motion (like a motor vehicle) is reluctant to deviate from its path; if left undisturbed it will tend to travel in a straight line and at a steady speed. This is known as *inertia*. Whenever we brake, accelerate or turn a corner, thus deviating from our existing state of motion, we experience inertia.

Inertia also applies to a body at rest, so that when we accelerate from a standstill, for example, we can sense that the vehicle is reluctant to move. It would prefer to remain stationary, but it is propelled forwards by the force of the engine. The tyres transmit the power of the engine to the ground, but because the centre of gravity of the car is a considerable distance above ground level, a moment (rotational motion, although you may prefer to think of it as a form of leverage) is created, so weight is transferred rearwards. The higher the C of G above ground level the greater the moment, and hence the greater the amount of weight transfer.

Because all conventional motor vehicles have some form of suspension, the weight transfer manifests itself in movement of the sprung mass, that part of the car that is supported by the springs – in simple terms, the body/chassis unit – and that is the sensation we feel, as to varying degrees this causes the rear springs to compress, the tail to squat and the nose of the vehicle to rise. We even feel the force of inertia acting on our own bodies; as the vehicle accelerates we tend to be 'left behind' and we experience this sensation as being pressed back in the seat.

Similarly, when the vehicle's brakes are operated, the braking force is applied by the tyres at ground level, but the car wants to carry on, so weight (acting through the C of G) is transferred forward, pushing the nose of the car down, compressing the front springs and in extreme cases throwing us forward against the seat belts. But don't be fooled into thinking the body movement *causes* weight transfer; it is merely a symptom of it. Even suspension-less vehicles – karts, for example – transfer weight under the forces of inertia. The only things that affect weight transfer are the height of the centre of gravity and the distance from the wheels, hence the further the wheels are from the C of G – *ie* the greater the track width and the longer the wheelbase – and the lower the centre of

The inertia we experience when accelerating hard results in squat, when the nose of the vehicle rises, and the tail dips, as a result of weight transfer rearwards.

Under heavy braking, the opposite happens: weight transfer causes the nose to dip, and the tail to rise. On a car with a pronounced forward weight bias, the front brakes may do 80% of the work of slowing the car . . . and perhaps even more.

gravity, the less the weight transfer. For reasons we will see later, keeping weight transfer to a minimum in cornering is A Good Thing, so the lower the C of G and the wider the track the better.

Centrifugal force

The inertia we experience in cornering is known as *centrifugal force*, and is familiar to all drivers. It is the force that tries to push a car away from the centre of a turn, as the car would prefer to continue in a straight line. The tyres provide an opposing force, and when the car is cornering under control the two forces are opposite and equal. If you want to be pedantic, the resisting force generated by the tyres is called centripetal force, although for convenience I will refer to it simply as cornering force. Centrifugal force (and therefore cornering force) is a function of corner radius, cornering speed and vehicle weight. The actual formula is:

$$\text{Centrifugal force} = \frac{\text{vehicle weight} \times \text{corner speed (mph)}^2}{14.97 \times \text{corner radius (ft)}}$$

Self evidently (because the speed must be determined), centrifugal force can only be established by empirical means – by testing in other words – and not by theoretical means of deduction or calculation. In fact the only way to measure the centrifugal force is to drive round a circle of known radius on a suitable stretch of tarmac as fast as possible (*ie* without running wide or spinning off) and time how long it takes to complete a 'lap', in order to determine speed.

When we put some figures into the equation we obtain a figure for centrifugal force in pounds (or kilogrammes if we prefer). The *lateral acceleration* is then derived by dividing the centrifugal force by the vehicle weight. If we take a 2000lb car that develops a centrifugal force of 1500lb, the lateral acceleration will be 0.75g, which in fact is a reasonably good performance for an ordinary passenger car on road tyres. The very best roadgoing high-performance sports cars, with tyres to match, may be able to generate 1.0g of lateral acceleration in ideal circumstances, while purpose-built racing cars, with inverted wings creating so-called downforce to force the tyres onto the road may, if the reports are to be believed, generate an incredible 2.0 to 3.0g, perhaps even more.

As we have seen, centrifugal force is a function of vehicle weight, corner radius

In cornering, weight transfer to the outside of the corner causes body roll. Most enthusiasts refer to this as centrifugal force although physics pedants will argue otherwise. Always remember though that this is the result of weight transfer . . . not the cause.

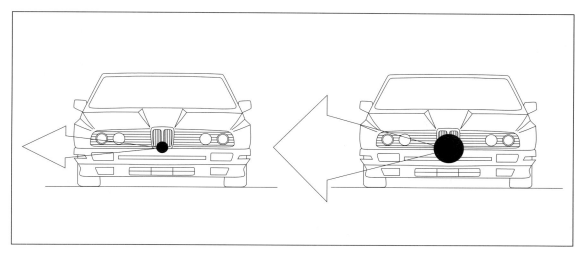

Illustration 1: The effect of vehicle weight
Centrifugal force is a function of vehicle weight, corner radius and speed. Therefore if you took two otherwise identical vehicles, one weighing 200kg more than the other (an unlikely scenario we know ... but bear with me), the heavier vehicle will generate more centrifugal force than the lighter one. Bearing in mind that cornering force and centrifugal force are equal when the vehicle is cornering under control, and that cornering force is limited – the tyres can only generate so much grip – then on a corner of a given radius, the heavier car will be slower than the lighter one when cornering on the limit.

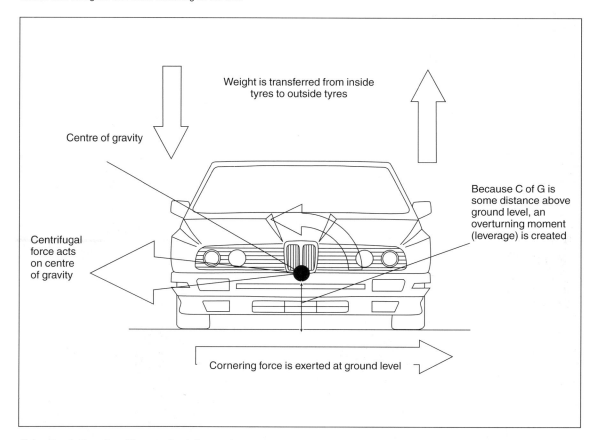

Illustration 2: Centrifugal force and weight transfer
In cornering, because centrifugal force exerts its pull on the centre of gravity of the vehicle (which is obviously at some considerable distance above the road surface) and because the tyres resist that force at ground level, an overturning moment is created. This causes weight to transfer from the inside to the outside tyres. It also causes body roll (but note that body roll does not cause weight transfer).

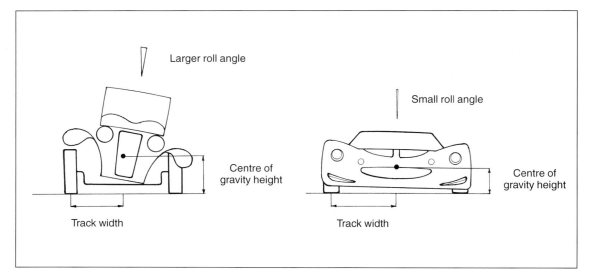

Illustration 3: Factors affecting weight transfer
The only factors that influence weight transfer are the weight of the vehicle itself, the height of the centre of gravity, and the distance of the centre of gravity from the tyre contact patches. That is, the longer the wheelbase, and the wider the track width, the less the weight transfer for a given amount of inertia. In cornering therefore, at a given speed on a given radius, a tall upright car will transfer more weight than a wide low-slung one. All other things being equal (which they seldom are of course!) it will also roll more. More crucially, maximum weight transfer (where the tyres attain their optimum slip angle, and therefore arrive at the limit of adhesion) will occur at considerably lower speed. But then, common sense could have told you that . . .

and speed. For any corner radius and speed, the greater the weight the higher the centrifugal force that must be resisted by the tyres, which is why heavier vehicles, like coaches and lorries, are more ponderous and are forced to corner more slowly; assuming a given corner radius, any increase in vehicle weight must be matched by a considerable reduction in corner speed if the equation is to balance. Conversely, a light car can corner faster than a heavier one, and therefore anything you can do to safely lighten your car will benefit cornering. For any given vehicle, though, the weight is fixed, so from the perspective of actually driving the car we can ignore weight as a factor. Therefore the only variables that matter are corner radius and speed: the higher the speed and the tighter the corner radius, the higher the centrifugal force.

Centrifugal force acts on the centre of gravity of the vehicle, and because it is resisted by the tyres at ground level the moment created causes weight to transfer to the outside tyres. Just as inertia causes squat under acceleration and nosedive under braking, centrifugal force causes the car body to roll, the loose change under

your seat to slide about and the kids to roll across the back seat, and prompts you to tilt your head and perhaps your entire upper body towards the inside of the corner.

Tyre slip

When we are driving fast on a circuit, whenever we wish to change course or speed (all of the time, in other words, as we should always be either accelerating, braking or cornering), we rely on the tyres to overcome inertia. The tyres therefore play a crucial role. We will examine this complex subject more fully in *Tyre Performance*, but for now, suffice to say that in order to develop any grip, either laterally (cornering force) or longitudinally (traction), tyres need to slip. Even when travelling at a steady speed in a straight line some tyre slip occurs, although this is so slight (perhaps 1% or even less) as to be indiscernible to the driver. Longitudinal slip can range therefore from almost zero to 100%, which equates to lock-up under braking or wheelspin under hard acceleration. Maximum traction, both in braking and acceleration, occurs at some modest percentage slip, usually in the range of 5-15%. That is why the maximum acceleration is achieved when the tyres are *just* spinning, and why the most effective braking is obtained when the wheels are only *just* allowed to continue rotating.

Cornering force

We are primarily concerned, however, with cornering force. In order to develop any cornering force tyres need to be turned at an angle to their direction of travel. The tyre, being elastic, distorts at the contact patch, and the angle thus formed between the direction in which the wheel (being rigid) is being steered and the direction in which it is actually travelling is known as the *slip angle*. The tyre clings to the road because the tread at the contact patch twists as it tries to align itself with the direction of travel.

The more the tyre is distorted the more tenaciously it clings to the road surface, and so cornering force rises with slip angle. As you might expect, though, there is a limit to how much the tyre can be distorted, and this is known as the *optimum slip angle*, which is where maximum cornering force is achieved. Usually this will fall within the range of 5-20deg, depending on the tyre design characteristics. Beyond the optimum slip angle, cornering force diminishes slightly at first, then drops rapidly as the tyre is distorted beyond its limit. As a generalization, the higher the performance capability of the tyre the smaller the optimum slip angle, so racing tyres and high-performance road tyres generally feature much stiffer construction (ultra-low profiles are an obvious manifestation of this) than everyday passenger car tyres in order to keep distortion to a minimum.

Three things influence the cornering force a tyre can produce: the coefficient of friction, the size of the contact patch and the weight it is carrying. The coefficient of friction depends on the interaction between the rubber and the road, and therefore depends on the abrasiveness of the road surface and the formulation of the rubber compound. We can't change the road surface (although of course we must remain aware of the possibility that it *can* change

unexpectedly, most commonly due to rain, or spilt oil and other fluids), and although it may be possible to change to tyres of a softer compound in order to obtain more grip, usually we will be working with a given tyre. The same applies to the size; we may be able to change to larger tyres offering a larger contact patch, but most of the time we have to work with what we have got.

In practical terms, therefore, the only variable that matters to us when driving is the weight on the tyre; this being the sum of the static weight plus any weight transfer caused by inertia (during acceleration or braking) or centrifugal force (in cornering). Why is the weight transfer so important? Because, as we have seen, the cornering force, or grip, generated by a tyre is largely dependent on the weight bearing down on it; the greater that weight the higher the pressure on each square inch of footprint, so the greater the cornering force the tyre will produce.

Remember that centrifugal force varies with weight, speed and corner radius. We know that we can ignore the effect of the static vehicle weight, as it cannot readily be changed. For any given corner, the radius is fixed, although we do of course try to make the radius as large as possible by using all of the road width on the entry and exit and 'cutting' the corner on the inside. So the only variable that really matters is speed; the faster we go through a corner of a given radius the more centrifugal force is generated and therefore the more weight will be transferred to the outside tyres.

Limit of adhesion

Logically enough, in order to cope with this increase in load the tyre also needs to work harder, so the slip angle increases. We know that increasing the vertical load on the tyre and increasing the slip angle both result in an increase in cornering force, but in what ratio or proportion is difficult to determine. No matter. The important point is that because of this, the increase in cornering force does not directly relate to the increase in weight; it is not a linear relationship because as load increases so does slip angle. As the load increases, therefore, cornering force increases, but not proportionally and – more to the point – not indefinitely. Eventually the tyre approaches its optimum slip angle where the greatest cornering force is produced. At that point we have reached the *limit of adhesion*.

Obviously this is a point of equilibrium, where weight transfer causes the tyre to assume its optimum slip angle, where maximum cornering force is obtained; in simple terms, the outside tyres are carrying the maximum load they can withstand while still maintaining their hold on the road. Any increase in speed, because it leads to an increase in centrifugal force, will result in an increase in weight transfer, which increases the slip angle still further, beyond the optimum slip angle; whereupon cornering force diminishes, slowly at first, then rapidly as the tyre relaxes its grip on the road altogether. The tyre begins to slide across the road surface and all the accepted rules of tyre behaviour are suspended as the tyre resumes its normal shape and the slip angle disappears. Grip is not lost altogether – otherwise control would be irretrievably lost whenever we exceed the optimum slip angle – but it is much reduced, which is why sliding the car through the corners, although it looks spectacular and feels fast, is slower than cornering at the limit of adhesion.

As an aside, that is why the four-wheel drift has all but disappeared from modern motor racing, to the chagrin of many fans. The best drivers are still operating right on the limit of adhesion, but because contemporary racing tyres – and high-performance road tyres come to that – use modern synthetic materials to stiffen the carcass, they operate at lower optimum slip angles, all but indiscernible to the naked eye. Modern racing cars, with the occasional exciting exception, appear to be cornering on rails. Nowadays, you need to go to an historic motor race meeting to see some big slip angles and spectacular tail-out cornering.

The four-wheel drift has all but disappeared from modern motor racing. If you want to see race cars sliding, you have to go to a vintage or classic race meeting, featuring cars like this.

Limiting weight transfer

Although I stated earlier that keeping weight transfer to a minimum is beneficial, it should be apparent that as a driver you can't do anything to reduce or minimize it if you are cornering at the limit of adhesion, as for reasons we have just seen, the limit of adhesion is effectively *defined* by the amount of weight transfer. However, if you are designing, building or modifying a car, anything you can do to reduce weight transfer – by reducing weight, lowering the C of G or widening the track width – will benefit cornering because a higher degree of centrifugal force will be required to achieve the same level of weight transfer. As the weight transfer is the limiting factor, more centrifugal force equals more speed!

Approaching the problem from the opposite direction, fitting wider, stickier tyres will allow more weight transfer before the limit of adhesion is reached. The only way to transfer more weight is to increase the centrifugal force, and again more centrifugal force equals more speed. To put this another way, bearing in mind that cornering force is equal to centrifugal force, the wider, stickier tyres allow more cornering force to be developed, thereby allowing you to negotiate a corner of given radius at higher speed.

Once you are driving the car on the track, however, the factors influencing cornering force and weight transfer are fixed and can therefore effectively be disregarded. The only thing that matters *to the driver*, therefore, for any given bend (bearing in mind that the corner radius is fixed) is the speed at which it is negotiated. So, armed with at least a rudimentary understanding of the forces acting on the vehicle at speed we can then take to the circuit and begin looking for the optimum line through the corners, and indeed around the entire circuit . . . an important distinction, as we shall see. And that is the subject of *The Right Line*.

In order to manage or control the weight transfer that occurs during cornering, braking and acceleration, the driver needs to operate the controls as smoothly as possible. Don't confuse smooth with slow though.

9

THE RIGHT LINE

Whenever enthusiasts gather to talk about cars and driving, sooner or later the conversation will turn to 'lines'. We talk about 'the line' around a circuit, or through a given corner. It should I hope be obvious that when we talk about lines we are talking about an idealized path through a corner, which we should attempt to follow. Sadly, perhaps, this mysterious line is not painted on the road; it is imaginary and can only be visualized as we approach and negotiate a corner. Nevertheless, the line is of crucial importance.

Centrifugal force again

In *Vehicle Dynamics* we examined the importance of centrifugal force and the way in which it causes weight to transfer to the outside tyres in cornering and how that in turn defines the limit of adhesion. Remember, the formula is:

$$\text{Centrifugal force} = \frac{\text{vehicle weight x corner speed (mph)}^2}{14.97 \text{ x corner radius (ft)}}$$

From this we can deduce that the key variables are corner radius, vehicle weight and speed. Usually, though, when we are considering a specific vehicle the weight will be fixed and so will the centrifugal force because it is determined by the cornering force the tyres are able to generate. The key variables, therefore, are speed and corner radius; the greater the corner radius the faster we can go.

Lateral acceleration

We can use simple mathematics to prove this. Because vehicle weight is a factor in calculating both centrifugal force and lateral acceleration we can eliminate this factor from both sides of the equation and obtain a simplified formula for lateral acceleration, which is:

$$\text{Lateral acceleration (in g)} = \frac{1.227 \text{ x radius}}{\text{time}^2}$$

Let's now put some numbers into the equation. It takes a very capable road car indeed to exceed 0.9g in lateral acceleration; most 'sporty' cars will fall in the range of 0.75 to 0.85g. Let us therefore assume a figure of 0.8g, and then, using schoolboy maths skills, we can establish that:

$$\frac{1.227}{0.8} = 1.538 = \frac{\text{radius}}{\text{time}^2}$$

Therefore:

$$\text{Time} = \sqrt{(\text{radius x } 1.538)}$$

If we assume a radius of 100ft, the time taken to do a full circle at 0.8g lateral acceleration will be 12.4secs ($\sqrt{153.8}$). Double the radius to 200ft and you double the distance travelled. The time taken will increase, naturally, to 17.54secs, but note that it doesn't double. Ergo, the speed — being a function of time to distance – will be greater. Indeed, we can calculate that our

The idea of using all of the road width, to make every corner radius as large as possible, is one of the most difficult for track day novices to grasp. You need a lot of confidence – preferably well founded! – in your own judgment, however, to do this consistently lap after lap. Novices should be prepared to 'sneak up' on the limits slowly, as mistakes can be severely punished.

hypothetical vehicle cornering at 0.8g can negotiate the 100ft radius circle at 34.55mph and the 200ft radius one at 48.85mph. Phew! That's a mighty long-winded way of proving what we knew all along . . .

The only reason to go through this exercise is to illustrate the point that the corner radius is a crucial element. It should be obvious, therefore, that when the lateral g the vehicle can generate is finite (and we will examine the reasons why in *Tyre Performance*), the greater the corner radius the higher the speed that can be maintained.

Using the road

It follows therefore that in order to take any given corner at the highest possible speed you need to make the radius as wide as possible. If you like, you need to straighten out the corner as much as possible. Imagine you are approaching a right-handed right-angle bend; you should approach on the left-hand side of the road, turn in at a point that allows you to clip the inside of the corner on the right-hand side of the road at the optimum point and sweep out to the edge of the road on the left-hand side as you exit the bend. Logically enough, those three points of reference are usually referred to as the turn-in point, the apex or clipping point, and the exit point. Thus you have used the full width of the road to make the corner radius as large as possible, and the path you have described in order to do so is 'the line'. The result of using the full road width can be seen in *Illustration 4*. This concept of 'using the road' is one of the most foreign and seemingly difficult to grasp for many track day novices, especially if they are disciplined road drivers who seldom if ever cross the centreline.

Joining the dots

At many track days the three points of reference – the turn-in, apex and exit points – may be marked by cones, which greatly simplifies learning any new circuit. Finding your way around a new circuit becomes like a glorified game of join-the-dots, with one important distinction: you are trying to connect the dots with a long, continuous, smoothly flowing line, not with a series of straight lines.

The key to achieving this 'flow' is to look well ahead. It is vital that you don't arrive at a 'dot' and then start looking for the next one: you should already know where it is. When you arrive at the turn-in cone, therefore, you should already be looking

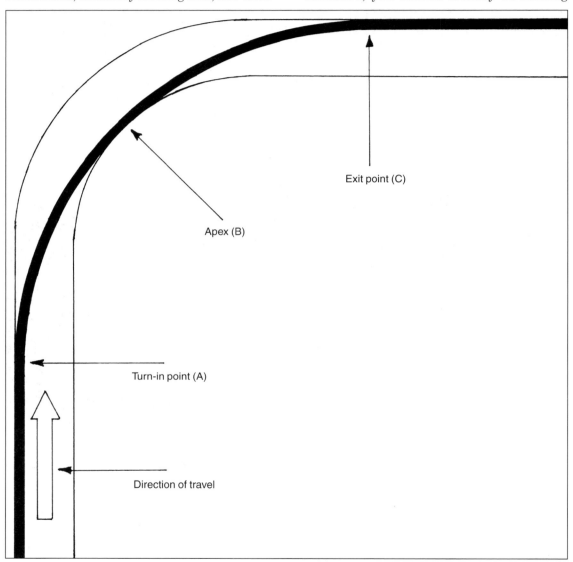

Illustration 4: Using the road width
Our imaginary 90deg bend has a nominal radius (to the centreline of the road) of 120ft, a road width of 40ft, and a vehicle width of 6ft. Assuming a cornering capability of 1.0g (a bit optimistic perhaps, but hey ... it makes the calculations simpler, okay?), then if you were to follow the centreline of the road (ie120ft corner radius) your speed would be 42.4mph. However, by using the road width to your advantage you can increase the corner radius to 215ft ... a huge difference that allows an increase in cornering speed to 56.7mph. Perhaps even more instructive is to consider what happens when you reduce the corner radius by just 2ft, meaning you turn in 1ft from the road edge, miss the apex by 1ft, and exit the corner with 1ft to spare. Corner speed would be reduced to 56.4mph, which may not sound like much, but would account for just under 0.3 of a second per circuit mile, a difference most racing drivers would kill for. While this clearly illustrates the importance of using all of the road, it also illustrates an even more important and little-understood fact: that when driving on the limit, you are working to very fine margins indeed, where the difference between too slow and too fast is measured in inches, and tenths of a mile per hour! Well, no-one said it was easy ...

When 'the line' through a corner is obscured by vegetation, Armco barriers, buildings, the natural topography of the circuit or whatever, you need to visualize the line instead. This becomes easier with practice.

towards the apex cone, and as you approach the apex cone your eyes should be scanning ahead, looking for the exit cone marking the edge of the circuit. Effectively you are looking two cones ahead, although that does not mean you can ignore the cone you are approaching. You cannot afford to turn in too early or too late, and you cannot afford to miss the apex, so in effect you need to look at both cones at once. In practice you achieve this by scanning rapidly from one to the other as frequently as you need to.

There is no point in looking only at the cone immediately in front of you because if you are travelling at speed you won't have time to spot the next cone and make the necessary steering input when you arrive at the cone: you won't be able to react quickly enough, and neither will the car! You should think in terms of aiming the car rather than steering it. The obvious corollary is that the faster you are travelling the further ahead you must look.

Visualization

Unfortunately there are places on many circuits where it is not possible to see far enough ahead. Your view may be obscured by the natural topography of the circuit, Armco barriers and tyre walls, buildings, trees or other vegetation, by a blind brow or simply because the corner is too long to see around fully. That is where visualization techniques come into play, where you have to imagine the line you need to steer, based on repetition and memory. Fortunately you can usually assume that the circuit conditions are unchanged from lap to lap, unless it starts to rain, of course.

Looking far enough ahead ensures that you are not only in the right place, but also at the right angle. You will eventually find that the turn-in cone tells you *where* to turn, the apex cone tells you *how much* to turn (assuming you have it fixed in your sights in time) and the exit cone is your cue to start unwinding the lock, allowing you to

accelerate onto the next straight. After a time you will find that you don't have to concentrate so hard on hitting (not literally!) the cones, and soon after that you will probably realize that you're not relying on the cones anymore. 'The line' will be starting to emerge . . .

Things become somewhat more complicated, though, when there are no cones to help you and you cannot benefit from someone else's hard-won skills and experience in determining where the cones should be placed. You then have to suss out the line for yourself. But before you can do that you need to know something about tyre performance and characteristics, which is the subject of *Tyre Performance*.

On very tight S-bends, such as here at Thruxton, the right line is effectively the only line, so even in a close-fought race the best policy is to form an orderly queue and plan to begin your overtaking manoeuvre as you exit. Track day drivers should do likewise.

10

TYRE PERFORMANCE

It should be apparent by now that the line you take through a corner, and indeed around the entire circuit, is crucial, as the right line is not only the fastest, but in most circumstances should also be the safest. Logically you might suppose that the best line through any given corner would be a geometrically perfect arc of the greatest possible radius. Indeed, if your purpose were to negotiate the corner as fast as possible it would be. But what you must never forget is that you are trying to negotiate *the entire circuit* as fast as possible, not just a single corner. For that reason you don't necessarily take the geometrically correct arc of greatest radius, and that is all because of the tyres.

In *Vehicle Dynamics* we have already looked at the importance of centrifugal force, a form of inertia that tries to push a car away from the centre of the turns. When we turn the steering wheel to negotiate a corner, the vehicle wants to remain on its original path, to continue straight ahead. The tyres generate a cornering force that opposes centrifugal force, and provided the car is cornering under control the two opposing forces are equal. Centrifugal force – resisted by the cornering force of the tyres – also results in weight transfer.

As we have seen, weight transfer occurs because the centrifugal force acts on the centre of gravity of the vehicle, which is obviously at some distance above the road surface, whereas the centripetal force resisting it occurs at the tyre contact patches, *ie* at the road surface. This creates an overturning moment (rotational motion, or leverage) that causes weight to transfer from the inside to the outside tyres in a corner, so that it is perfectly possible for the outside tyres to be carrying 80% of the total vehicle weight, or perhaps even more. Indeed, you occasionally see cars actually rise up onto two wheels when they are cornered a bit too enthusiastically so that the outside wheels are doing 100% of the work, although that is clearly not a desirable state of affairs and usually hints at a handling problem.

Under more normal circumstances, the outside tyres are providing most of the grip, with the inside tyres making a minor contribution to overall cornering force. When we talk about the tyres, therefore, and the loads imposed on them during cornering, it is safe to assume we are referring to the outside tyres.

Slip angle
In order to develop any cornering force, tyres need to be turned at an angle to their actual direction of travel. Tyres are flexible and so they distort, most significantly at the point of contact with the road, so the direction of travel is different to the direction the wheel itself (being rigid) is pointing. You can liken this to an aircraft flying in a strong crosswind, in which the

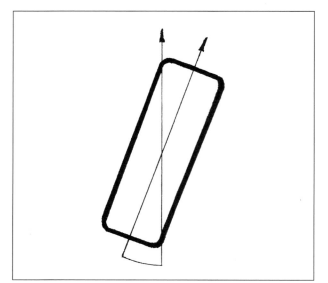

Illustration 5: Generating cornering force
In order to generate any lateral grip (cornering force) a tyre must be turned at an angle to its actual direction of travel. The difference between the angle steered and the actual direction of travel is the slip angle, and the difference is accounted for by distortion of the tyre tread at the contact patch. An amusing corollary is that a tyre will not generate any cornering force without adopting a slip angle, but it will not adopt a slip angle without generating some cornering force. Go figure . . .

heading (the direction the aircraft is pointing) is different to the track (the path it is actually following). You can actually observe this distortion, or twisting of the tyre tread, if you attempt to turn the steering wheel when stationary; although being knowledgeable and mechanically sympathetic drivers none of us ever do this, do we? If we were to do so, though (on a purely experimental basis of course!), we would also be able to feel through the rim of the steering wheel how strenuously the tyre resists this attempt to twist it. The tyre clings to the road because the tyre tread at the contact patch twists to align itself with the direction of travel.

The driver initiates this distortion of the tyre when he first turns the steering wheel. This difference in angle, between the direction the tyre is aimed and the path it is actually following, is called the slip angle. Although it may be difficult to envisage, when we turn the steering wheel to initiate cornering, the rear tyres simultaneously also assume a slip angle. The curious paradox to this is that tyres don't develop a slip angle without generating some grip, and they don't develop any grip without developing some slip angle. Every time we deviate from the straight-ahead we generate a slip angle in the tyres, as a result of which they then produce the grip needed to keep us on our intended course (usually!).

Optimum slip angle

The relationship between cornering force and slip angle is a curious one in that cornering force rises with slip angle, and slip angle rises with cornering force: they are like flip sides of the same coin if you like. However, there is naturally a limit to how much distortion a tyre will tolerate and hence there is an *optimum slip angle*, where maximum cornering force is achieved. When we corner gently, the slip angle in a road tyre may be only one or two degrees. The faster we corner, the harder the tyre needs to work, the more it is distorted by the loads imposed on it, and the greater the slip angle it develops. Cornering force (grip) rises with slip angle up to a peak, beyond which it falls away rapidly. We can plot the relationship of grip to slip angle on a graph, and the curve will look something like that in *Illustration 6*. From that we can see there is an optimum slip angle, where maximum grip is obtained; go beyond it, and grip begins to fall, then drops dramatically.

The shape of the curve will be similar for virtually all tyres; only the scales will be different. For racing tyres, grip levels will be higher, the slope of the curve may be steeper, and the optimum slip angle may be in the range of 5-10deg, as racing tyres tend to be much stiffer in construction (ride comfort is not a consideration) and consequently operate at lower slip angles than road tyres, whose optimum slip angle may lie in the range of 8-20deg.

Illustration 7 shows a comparison between a normal passenger car tyre, a high-performance road tyre and a racing tyre. As a generalization, the higher the performance of the tyre, the lower the optimum slip angle. Please note, however, that these are entirely hypothetical curves, devised for illustration purposes only (hard information about tyre performance characteristics is commercially sensitive and jealously guarded by the tyre manufacturers, and hence notoriously difficult to come by).

Clearly then, the key to obtaining maximum tyre performance is to ensure that the tyres are operating at the optimum slip angle as much as possible. The driver, however, has no means of seeing or measuring the slip angle; the actual value, therefore, is of largely academic interest to him. He is relying on the feel the tyres give him through his contact points with the car: the seat and the steering wheel. That feel is provided by the tyres' self-aligning torque.

Self-aligning torque
Logically enough, the tyres do not take too kindly to being distorted to the optimum slip angle. They resist this distortion, setting up a force known to tyre engineers as self-aligning torque, which is self-explanatory; the tyre tries to pull itself back into its regular shape. Broadly

Illustration 6: Passenger car tyre characteristics
Hypothetical curve of slip angle against coefficient of friction for a typical passenger car tyre, showing a maximum c/f of around 0.8 (the coefficient of friction is a measure of the tyre's grip potential, derived by dividing the cornering force it will generate by the weight resting on it), a gentle upward slope towards the maximum c/f, and a broad range of slip angles (say, 10-18deg) where the maximum coefficient of friction is produced. This produces a tyre with very benign characteristics, ideal for the ordinary motorist who may seldom venture onto the upper slopes of the curve. Such a tyre has relatively little grip, and will give plenty of warning when approaching the limit of adhesion, with a broad plateau at the limit, making it extremely forgiving. For the sporting motorist though, the responses will seem altogether too soft and sluggish.

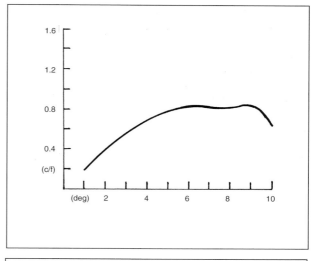

Illustration 7: Characteristics of normal, high-performance road and race tyres compared
The characteristics of the passenger car tyre are as described above (Illustration 6). The race tyre, by comparison, has a much steeper slope, so will offer much faster response. The obvious corollary is that it will give the driver less warning as it approaches the limit, and also offers a much narrower range of slip angles (say, 7-10deg) at the limit of adhesion (maximum c/f). With a maximum c/f approaching 1.4, it will generate huge amounts of grip, but it will be much harder to feel the limit approaching, and (because of the smaller plateau) harder to keep it at the limit. More or less as you would expect really. The high-performance road car tyre falls somewhere between the two: maximum c/f around 1.0, maintained over 7-12deg slip angle.

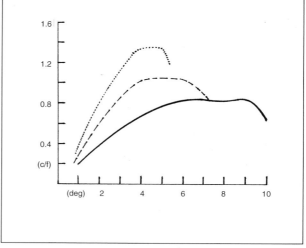

The modern high-performance tyre is a marvel. Materials and construction methods in current use – including ultra-low profile construction – mean that slip angles are kept to a minimum. Yet grip levels are superb.

rises too steeply, or if the peak is too sharp, then it is difficult for the driver to feel when the tyre may be approaching the limit of adhesion; therefore it is beneficial if the curve rises gradually, with a reasonably broad plateau at the top to allow the driver to stay at or near the top of the curve more easily. If taken too far, however, the curve can be made too benign, in which case the tyre may feel sloppy and unresponsive. As always, you can't have it all ways!

When the tyre has a broad range of slip angles at or near the top of the curve – usually regarded as a desirable characteristic – you will notice that within that range any increase in slip angle produces only a negligible increase in cornering force. In other words, at 15 degrees of slip angle there is little more grip than at 10deg. But there is a great deal more drag, which slows you down; and there is also a good deal more heat build-up, which may in time cause the tyres to overheat and 'go off'. Clearly, therefore, it is preferable to use 10deg of slip angle rather than 15deg when there is little to be gained from using the higher figure. The optimum slip angle, therefore, will be the minimum slip angle that gives the greatest lateral acceleration, or the most grip for the least drag in other words.

Factors affecting cornering force

If we want to develop more cornering force there are only three ways of doing so. First is to increase the friction between road and tyre; either by a softer tread compound or a more abrasive – usually coarser – road surface. The second way is to put more rubber on the road, the most obvious way being to use a wider tyre offering a broader contact patch, although a taller tyre, resulting in a longer contact patch, is also a possibility. For a given car on a given circuit, however, we can assume these to be fixed: you have a certain road surface to work with and a given wheel and tyre combination, neither of which you can readily change. I am also assuming that the tyre is working properly; *ie* that the dampers and springs, the static suspension settings and tyre pressures are sorted, so the tyre is being kept in contact with the

speaking, the greater the slip angle the greater the self-aligning torque, but then, as the tyre approaches the optimum slip angle, a curious thing happens; the self-aligning torque peaks *before* the tyre reaches the optimum slip angle, and then begins to decline. This allows the driver to feel the approach of the limit of adhesion as the tyres begin to behave subtly differently. The difference is virtually impossible to describe. The nearest I can come to describing this sensation is that everything starts to feel *lighter* somehow; the steering may feel lighter, and the rear tyres may feel as though they are not clinging to the road quite so tenaciously . . . which of course is precisely the case. Sensing the approach of the limit of adhesion is one of the skills you must acquire if you are to drive fast in safety on a race circuit, and the most skilled drivers clearly have a very finely attuned feel for this.

If the cornering force/slip angle curve

At the limit of adhesion, lateral weight transfer causes the vertical load on the heavily loaded outside tyres to increase. This has the effect of increasing their slip angle, until the optimum slip angle is achieved. A state of equilibrium then exists, which is easily disturbed by clumsy driver inputs, or external factors like severe bumps in the road, wet or oily patches of tarmac, or abrupt changes in gradient.

ground as much as possible, and as nearly as possible at the right angle in cornering (perpendicular or perhaps up to 1deg negative camber) and within the right temperature range. That being so, the only real variable that influences grip is the vertical load (the weight, if you like) on the tyre.

You might assume the weight pressing the tyre on the road is fixed, being some proportion of the overall weight of the vehicle. That is true so long as the vehicle remains stationary. But of course, as we have seen in *Vehicle Dynamics*, the weight varies constantly once the vehicle is in motion due to the effect of weight transfer under acceleration, braking and cornering. Although longitudinal weight transfer has an influence, for the time being we will concern ourselves only with lateral weight transfer.

Complex relationship

There is a complex and dynamic relationship between vertical load (weight) on the tyre, cornering force (or grip) and slip angle. The more vertical load on a tyre

(static load plus the additional load imparted by weight transfer) the more cornering force it will generate. This is logical enough as the unit pressure on the tyre footprint is greater, *ie* it is being pressed onto the ground harder. Think of a rubber pencil eraser, and imagine rubbing it across a smooth surface: the harder you press down on it the more it resists being dragged across the surface. You may also notice that the greater this resistance (the eraser's equivalent of cornering force) the more the eraser distorts. Tyres, being elastic, also distort, and they react in the same way as our eraser: the greater the load the greater the distortion. In the case of the tyre, this distortion takes the form of an increase in slip angle, therefore every increase in vertical load also increases the slip angle.

As we have seen, increasing the vertical load on the tyre and increasing the slip angle both result in an increase in cornering force, but the increase in cornering force does not directly relate to the increase in weight; it is not a linear relationship because as load increases so does slip angle. As the load increases, therefore, so does cornering force, but not proportionally and – more to the point – not indefinitely. Eventually the tyre, in response to the increase in load, approaches its optimum slip angle, where the greatest cornering force is produced. At that point, you will recall, we have reached the *limit of adhesion*.

Equilibrium

At the limit of adhesion (maximum cornering force), the tyre will be working at the optimum slip angle for the vertical load it is carrying, that being the static weight *plus* the weight transferred to the outside tyre under the influence of centrifugal force. In simple terms, therefore, the weight transfer to the outside tyres is the ultimate determinant of cornering speed. Remember that the amount of weight transfer in a corner is determined by the centrifugal force generated (a function of speed and corner radius, ignoring for convenience the weight of the vehicle itself, as that cannot be changed) and the vehicle's centre of gravity height and track width. On any corner of a given radius, therefore, at the limit of adhesion there exists a very fine state of equilibrium between the vertical load on the tyre caused by weight transfer, tyre slip angle and speed.

That is why when you are cornering on the limit, a severe bump in the road can have such an unsettling effect as it causes a sudden increase in vertical load on the tyre, albeit in the opposite direction (*ie* the road pushing against the tyre, rather than the tyre pressing down on the road). Usually most of this will be absorbed by the springs, but some small increase in load on the tyre is inevitable. The effect will be felt most dramatically if the extra compression causes the springs to bind, or the suspension to contact the bump stops. This may be enough to cause the tyre to exceed the optimum slip angle, and a slide or skid, perhaps even complete loss of control, is the likely result.

Similarly, abrupt steering movements, causing an increase in slip angle, can take the tyre beyond its optimum slip angle,

resulting in a sudden and dramatic loss of cornering force; again, a slide is the likely outcome. This is also why you sometimes see race cars spin wildly out of control after the faintest touch with another competitor, often gentle enough to leave both machines completely unmarked.

Likewise any increase in speed, because it leads to an increase in centrifugal force, will result in an increase in weight transfer, which increases the slip angle still further, beyond the optimum slip angle. At this point cornering force diminishes, slowly at first, and then rapidly as the tyre relaxes its grip on the road altogether until it is just being dragged bodily across it. What happens in fact is that the tyre abruptly resumes its normal shape, the slip angle disappears and the tyre slides instead of grips. It still has some grip of course, but this is entirely due to friction between the road surface and the tread, which in extreme cases results in the rubber tearing off the tread, hence the black lines left on the road by a skidding or sliding tyre. Sliding wildly, while it looks spectacular and feels fast, is slower than keeping the tyres operating at the optimum slip angle and at the limit of adhesion.

The reduction in cornering force is clearly illustrated when you see a car spin out of control on a race track. As it spins it slows down, but note how much speed must be lost before the driver can regain control; usually it will be down to a quarter or perhaps a third of its usual speed at that point before the driver can gather it up again. Indeed, if the initial spin is especially violent (perhaps after a nudge from another vehicle), it seems that the car will continue to spin almost indefinitely, and sometimes you will see a car that appears, briefly, to be back under control spin again for no apparent reason, often at ludicrously low speed.

Trading traction for cornering force

Having established these broad principles, how do the tyres affect the line we choose to take through the corners? Well, tyres are a bit like human beings in that they don't like doing two things at once. You know what it's like when you're on the telephone and

And this is the result. Once that delicate balance has been lost, the car must shed a lot of speed before control can be regained. On the race track – especially on a high-speed oval – you may see cars continue to spin, often at comically low speeds.

someone bursts into the room and fires a question at you? Usually you'll either have to ask your caller to hold the line for a moment and deal with the interruption, or ask the person who has just come in to wait until you've finished your call. That's because we find it difficult to concentrate on both conversations at once. Tyres are a bit like that. They don't like braking hard and cornering hard at the same time; or cornering hard and accelerating flat out at the same time (hopefully you won't be asking them to brake and accelerate at the same time!).

This is because, when the tyre is operating at the optimum slip angle, it is by definition giving the maximum grip available and therefore there is no further grip available for acceleration or braking. In other words, the tyres have a finite amount of grip and traction available, which must be shared between the three modes; braking, cornering (either left or right) and acceleration (traction), so you need to trade off grip in one mode to allow some in another. Therefore, in order to

allow the tyre to generate some traction (*ie* longitudinal grip for either acceleration or braking), we need to reduce the slip angle of the tyre by reducing the cornering force.

Bearing in mind that cornering force and centrifugal force are equal, and remembering that centrifugal force is a function of vehicle weight, speed and corner radius, it should be apparent that we can do this (given that the vehicle weight is fixed) either by slowing down or making the corner radius greater. Which do you think we try to do?

Obviously, we should try to make the corner radius larger. In practical terms, that means reducing the amount of steering lock you have applied to reduce the slip angle, so reducing the lateral (cornering) load on the tyres, in order to free up some of their grip for acceleration. Similarly, if you want or need to brake into a corner (because the braking area is on a curve, for example) you need to ease off the brakes slightly in order to allow the tyres to generate a little lateral grip at the same time. If the braking area curves more acutely you may have to exercise great finesse, and brake very gently and subtly in order to retain enough cornering grip to hold your chosen line.

Anti-lock braking

Indeed, that is what anti-lock braking (ABS) achieves, by reducing the braking effort so the wheels are *just* prevented from locking. Most keen drivers will know that the tyres do not grip effectively when the brakes are locked on: all that happens is that the tyre patches in contact with the road very quickly overheat drastically and the car slides on the molten rubber, which is why the tyres develop flat spots if you have a serious lock-up. It is vital that the tyres are *just* kept rotating, so that they are operating at 5-15% slip, the optimum value for efficient retardation. Cadence braking – pumping the brake pedal rapidly – achieves much the same effect, slowing the car as quickly as feasible by ensuring that the wheels are kept rotating. But you need skill and considerable presence of mind to cadence brake in a genuine emergency, not least because it happens but rarely – at least to a skilled and vigilant driver – so there is seldom any opportunity to practice. Experience is a good teacher.

Contrary to popular belief, ABS does not *necessarily* allow shorter braking distances (although it may do, largely because few average road drivers have the skill to brake hard without locking up, or to cadence brake), but it does allow the driver to *retain steering control* during hard braking, most especially in an emergency. That is the *real* benefit of ABS.

If you have ever locked the brakes in an emergency you will know that the car simply does not respond to the steering; it will simply plough on in the original direction of travel. That is because all of the available tyre grip – what we call the total traction capability – is being used for braking, leaving nothing available for steering. However, with electronically controlled ABS the computer repeatedly and very rapidly compares the rotational speeds of all four wheels, and if one stops rotating, the computer reduces brake line pressure to ensure that it keeps rolling. This happens so rapidly it is all but indiscernible to the driver because the wheel never actually stops turning; the computer works so quickly it senses incipient rather than actual lock-up. The pulsing you may feel at the brake pedal when the ABS is working is the system modulating the brake pressure to prevent lock-up, although this is not something I recommend you make a habit of experiencing: frequent resort to ABS is a sure sign of poor observation and anticipation!

It is an unfortunate dichotomy of ABS that without it you need to brake with the utmost sensitivity and skill in an emergency, whereas an ABS-equipped vehicle must be braked *hard* for the ABS to take over. If you try to modulate the braking effort yourself you will simply negate the benefit of ABS. Trust it; just stand on the middle pedal as hard as you can, and don't forget to steer (don't laugh . . . many people 'freeze' in an emergency) if that looks a better option to keep you out of trouble. However, if you do steer during an emergency stop you won't slow down as quickly because the tyres have to surrender a little braking grip to allow some cornering, so even though the ABS is doing the hard work you still need to think and react quickly to decide on your best course of action: stop or steer. This is no problem if you always drive a car with (or without!) ABS, but if you routinely drive different cars it may behove you to make a mental note every time you set off so that you may respond appropriately if required. Clearly, though, it is preferable to avoid emergencies altogether!

But enough talk about slowing down; what about going faster? Under acceleration the same general principle applies; by reducing the tyre slip angle and trading a little lateral (cornering) grip for longitudinal grip (traction), you will be able to accelerate harder and earlier. That is the key to fast lap times, and it is the subject of the next chapter, *Maximum Acceleration*.

11

MAXIMUM ACCELERATION

In normal circumstances, unless you are driving something monstrously powerful, accelerating in a straight line presents no real control difficulties. It is only when you are accelerating out of a corner that you are likely to encounter problems. As we have seen in *Tyre Performance*, your car's tyres have only so much grip available, and it must be apportioned between accelerating and cornering: accelerate too hard when the tyre is still being asked to transmit a lot of cornering force and you will exceed the tyre's total traction capability, they will give up in disgust and the wheels will spin.

The same applies if you exceed the limits of adhesion in cornering or braking. Whether the tyres are locked up under braking, sliding bodily sideways in a corner or spinning wildly as a result of too much accelerator, they are no longer clinging to the road but being dragged bodily across it, relying only on friction between the tread and the road surface; they will not grip as efficiently as when the tyre is rolling and generating a slip angle.

Importance of acceleration

Your objective, therefore, should be to achieve the maximum acceleration out of the corner without exceeding the total traction capability of the tyres. By reducing the tyre slip angle and trading a little lateral (cornering) grip for longitudinal grip (traction) you will be able to accelerate harder and earlier, which is the key to fast

lap times; the sooner and harder you can accelerate out of a corner the faster you will be on the straight that follows. Contrary to popular belief it is not tearing around the corners as fast as possible that gets you around the circuit fastest, nor is it braking at the last possible moment; the quickest way is to go down the *straights* as fast as possible, which means leaving the corners and hence entering the straights as fast as possible.

This is why race teams will always aim to gear their cars to achieve maximum rpm in top gear at the fastest point on the circuit, usually the very end of the longest straight. It ensures that the car will always be accelerating, whereas if the gearing is too short the engine will reach maximum rpm before the end of the straight, wasting acceleration potential. Conversely, if the gearing is too tall the engine cannot achieve maximum rpm in top gear so, again, some acceleration potential is being squandered. Of course, the optimum gearing is sometimes difficult to achieve, in which case some compromise may prove necessary.

A road car's gearbox typically will have a very low first gear in order to allow easy hill starts and perhaps to allow for towing a trailer . . . or even the odd hill start while towing a trailer! Conversely, fifth gear in most road cars is tall to allow relaxed motorway cruising with minimal fuel consumption, low noise levels and reduced

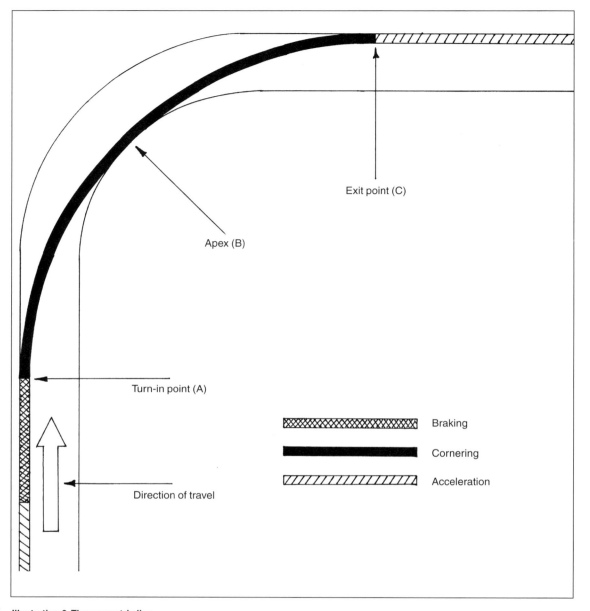

Exit point (C)

Apex (B)

Turn-in point (A)

⊠⊠⊠⊠⊠⊠⊠⊠⊠⊠⊠⊠⊠⊠ Braking

▬▬▬▬▬▬▬▬▬▬▬▬▬ Cornering

//////////////// Acceleration

Direction of travel

Illustration 8: The geometric line
By taking the geometric line, we achieve the greatest possible corner radius, and hence the highest achievable speed (in this case, with a corner radius of 215ft and a vehicle capable of cornering at 1.0g, 56.7mph) through the corner. That would be great if our objective was to get around the corner as fast as possible, but we must never forget that our objective is to get around the entire circuit as quickly as possible...

wear and tear. Most road cars therefore have a first gear that is unnecessarily short in normal road driving and ridiculously short for circuit use, widely spaced intermediate ratios offering great flexibility, and a tall fifth gear that can be used only briefly, if at all, on the circuit. The ideal for the circuit is a tall first gear, a short fifth and three ultra-close ratios in between to maximize acceleration; clearly the two are fundamentally incompatible. A gearbox optimized for circuit use will prove a difficult proposition on the road, and if you use your normal road car for track days, once again you may need to compromise.

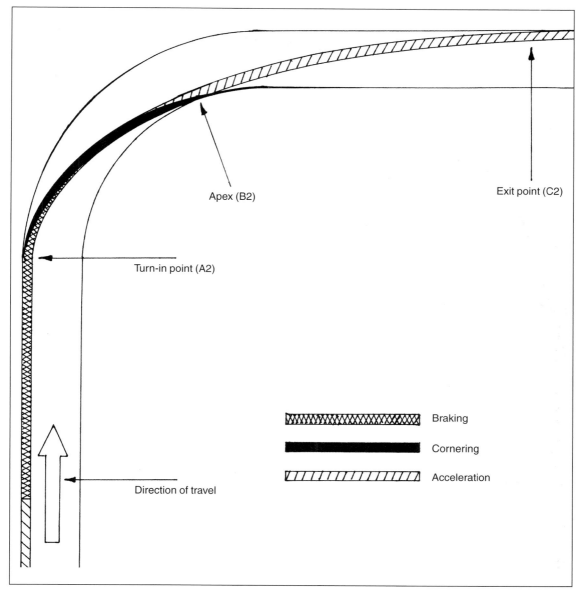

Apex (B2)

Exit point (C2)

Turn-in point (A2)

| Braking |
| Cornering |
| Acceleration |

Direction of travel

Illustration 9: The acceleration line
A tight initial turn followed by a gradual 'opening out' of the corner allows early acceleration and hence the optimum speed along the straight that follows. Note that tighter turn-in means speed at turn-in must be slower than turn-in for the geometric line, but this is more than compensated at corner exit . . . and all the way along the straight that follows. Note also that later turn-in means the braking area is longer, so braking can start at the same point, or possible even slightly later. The apex or clipping point is much further around corner than the geometric apex.

If you have a dedicated track day vehicle and if performance parts for it are readily available you may be able to gear it for greater acceleration, which will markedly improve its performance, although this is by no means essential. However, if you use your vehicle on the road and/or if there is no close-ratio gearset readily available, simply concentrate on enjoying it and getting the most from it just as it is.

I should perhaps clarify that when I refer to a straight I don't mean the road necessarily has to be geometrically straight; I mean any stretch of circuit that is straight enough to allow you to use full

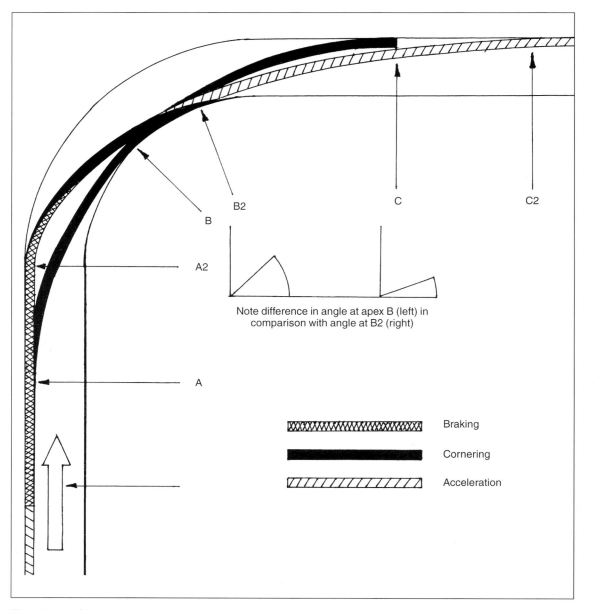

B2

B

A2

A

C

C2

Note difference in angle at apex B (left) in
comparison with angle at B2 (right)

XXXXXXXXXXXXXXXXXXXXXXXXX Braking

Cornering

/////////// Acceleration

Illustration 10: Comparison of geometric line and acceleration line

When we overlay the geometric line and the acceleration line, the differences are clearly apparent. (In fact, the differences have been grossly exaggerated for clarity. In reality, the differences – both in the line taken and in the relative speeds – will be much less.) In this example, I have calculated that at 1.0g, you could teeter around our corner of 215ft radius at 56.7mph, following the line of maximum constant radius. You will be travelling at 56.7mph all the way through the corner from the turn-in point (A), past the apex (B), until the exit point (C). Because you are using the entire available tyre grip for cornering, you will not be able to accelerate until you get to point C. But by making a slower, tighter turn in the early part of the corner, you can take a late apex and 'open out' the second part of the corner to reduce the tyre slip angle and free-up a little tyre grip for acceleration. In order to achieve this you increase the corner radius coming out of the turn, and the only way to do so is to reduce the corner radius at the beginning of the turn. Thus you turn in later at A2, and in order to hit the later apex at B2 you will need to apply more lock and turn more sharply, so obviously you will need to slow down more, to, say, 50mph. You might assume you will need to commence braking earlier, but in fact, by turning in later you have effectively made the braking area longer, so in practice it makes little or no difference to where you start braking. By the time you reach the later apex at B2 you have already turned through, say, 65-70deg (as opposed to 45deg on the geometric line), and you can progressively wind-off steering lock and apply the throttle. By B2 you should be on full throttle, or very nearly so, so that by the time you get adjacent to point C (bearing in mind that you will be on a somewhat different line, aiming to exit the corner much further along the straight, at point C2) you may have accelerated to 60mph . . . perhaps even 65 or 70mph. At the same point, the driver taking the 'classic' line is still doing 56.7mph. Guess who gets to the other end of the straight first? Yes, if you can come out of a corner going faster than the other guy, it's like having a head start. Most importantly of all, that advantage is maintained all the way along the straight that follows. The longer the straight, the greater the advantage.

throttle. It should be apparent that the straights (*ie* the full-throttle sections) constitute by far the greatest portion of the lap, even on a tight and twisty circuit. When your objective is to go fast the more time you spend on full throttle the better. If you can go down the straights faster than everybody else you will complete the lap in less time. Everything you do, therefore, should be predicated towards accelerating as soon as possible, as hard as possible and for as long as possible.

Slow in – fast out

This means you sometimes have to sacrifice a little speed going into a corner in order to gain speed coming out. Most enthusiasts will be familiar with the concept of 'slow in – fast out'. In order to illustrate this, let us refer again to our simple 90deg corner with 120ft radius (*Illustration 8*). Using the equation reproduced in *The Right Line*, we can establish that at the limit of adhesion, and assuming (for convenience) a cornering capability (lateral acceleration) of 1.0g, our speed would be limited to 56.7mph. Therefore you will be travelling at 56.7mph all the way through the corner from the entry point A, past the apex point B until the exit point C. Because you are using the entire available tyre grip for cornering you will not be able to accelerate until you get to point C.

Let us now consider what happens if you take the 'slow in – fast out' approach (*Illustration 9*). By making a slower, tighter turn in the early part of the corner you can take a late apex and 'open out' the second part of the corner to reduce the slip angle of the tyres and thus free up a little tyre grip for acceleration. In order to achieve this you increase the corner radius coming out of the turn, and the only way to do this is to reduce the radius at the beginning of the turn. Looking at our diagram, you turn in later at A2, and in order to hit the later apex B2 you will need to apply more lock and turn more sharply, so obviously you will need to slow down more. By the time you reach B2, however, you have turned through 65-70deg and you can apply full throttle and start to unwind the steering. *Illustration 10* compares the two approaches

and clearly illustrates the benefits of the Acceleration Line.

A head start

Assuming cars of roughly equal performance, that head start will enable you to breeze past on any reasonable-length straight and/or make it very difficult for anyone to overtake you. It is impossible to quantify, but you would need *a lot* of extra horsepower to overcome that deficit on any reasonable-length straight. In reality, the difference in exit speed will be very much smaller – 2 or 3mph would be a handy margin – but the principle remains the same.

In attempting to achieve maximum acceleration out of a corner we will be constantly assessing the total traction available and calculating the desired balance between traction and cornering grip. Luckily we have access to the most sophisticated computer known to man, the human brain! Because we are fallible, however, sooner or later we will get it wrong.

When things go wrong

Given that there is a delicate balance between cornering force and traction, it is very easy to exceed the tyres' total traction capability by pressing the loud pedal a bit too enthusiastically and spinning the wheels. Indeed, you may not even need to spin the wheels in order to exceed the tyres' total traction capability. Remember the effect of longitudinal weight transfer under acceleration. This will take weight off the front tyres and add it to the rears, and this addition of weight to the rear tyres may take them beyond their optimum slip angle and therefore exceed their limit of adhesion.

The first and obvious thing to do when this happens is to reduce power to restore traction, which means lifting off the throttle. It is important, though, that this is done smoothly, not abruptly. It may also be preferable not to lift off the throttle completely; a smidgen of throttle will help to keep the vehicle stable. Simply easing smoothly off the throttle may be enough to restore traction and stability to a front-

Once the tyre's total tractive capability has been exceeded, for example when excessive accelerator has been applied, there will be no cornering force available; traction for acceleration will also be compromised.

wheel-drive car, which is arguably more forgiving in this respect, hence why front-wheel-drive is favoured by most of the world's major motor manufacturers. Oh . . . and the fact that's it's cheaper to build of course!

With a rear-wheel-drive car, feeding a surfeit of power to the rear wheels will break adhesion, resulting in a rear-wheel slide, also known as power oversteer. To maintain control, first you need to steer into the slide by reducing the steering lock, and perhaps even applying a little opposite lock. Opinions vary, though, as to what you should do with the accelerator pedal. Some argue that you should keep the power on, whereas others figure that as your big right foot is what got you into trouble in the first place, a little less of it is what is needed. I am inclined to subscribe to the latter view. If you decide to lift off the throttle, though, in the case of rear-wheel drive it is even more imperative to do this smoothly, and preferably to keep some power going to the rear wheels. If you lift off the throttle abruptly the car could snap the other way, which will almost invariably result in a loss of control. For more on this see *Steering Techniques*.

Minimizing tyre slip angle

Your guiding principle should always be to maximize acceleration. In order to achieve this you need to minimize the tyre slip angle, for two reasons. One is to allow the tyre to develop some traction for acceleration, so you have to sacrifice some cornering force. The second is that whenever a tyre has a slip angle it also generates considerable drag. To prove the significance of this, try doing a coast-down test in a straight line, then – being careful to ensure your own safety and that of others – try it on a curve and observe how much more quickly the car sheds speed. That is the effect of drag, or tyre scrub, and it seriously hinders acceleration. Remember that grip equates to drag, and to achieve the maximum acceleration and hence speed you need as little drag as possible.

Smooth gearchanges

When you are operating at the limit of adhesion you must try to keep the flow of power to the wheels as smooth as possible. If you find you are approaching maximum engine speed when accelerating hard out of a corner and you need to change up, it is important to keep your gearchanges smooth and avoid jerkiness. The slower your starting speed the more difficult this becomes. The most difficult change to get right is first into second, for two reasons.

First, the torque multiplication is greatest in first gear, therefore the torque reversal when you lift off the throttle is also greater. For the same reason, the rate of acceleration is greatest in first gear and, conversely, the rate of deceleration when coasting in gear will also be greatest. That makes it imperative to co-ordinate pedal movement and time your gearshift perfectly to avoid jerkiness. If you lift off the throttle before you depress the clutch, the torque reversal will cause the car to slow suddenly, almost as though you had tapped the brake pedal, which inevitably will result in a snatched, jerky gearchange. Conversely, if you depress the clutch fractionally before lifting off the throttle you obviously risk over-revving the motor. Getting it exactly right takes skilled synchronization in operating the clutch and accelerator.

The second reason is that the rpm drop will be greatest between first and second, perhaps as much as 3000rpm. For example, if we change gear at 7000rpm in first the engine speed will drop to 4000rpm when we engage second, whereas when we change from fourth to fifth the rpm drop may be only 500 to 600rpm. In the lower gears especially, therefore, you have to release the clutch smoothly to take up the drive without snatching. One useful trick is to avoid lifting completely off the throttle so the engine does not drop all the way back to idle speed. Indeed, if you were to hold the engine at 4000rpm in our earlier example your gearchange should be seamless.

In order to achieve the desired perfect co-ordination of clutch, throttle and gearshift it may help to slow down your gearchanges. As in all aspects of fast driving, if you work on developing smoothness, speed will automatically follow. When you develop the smoothness necessary for fast progress on the race circuit, not just in gearchanging but in all aspects of driving, it will benefit your road driving immensely. Thankfully, this is something you can safely, practicably and

Unlike many other techniques used on track days, smooth gearchanging can safely and beneficially be practised in normal road driving.

beneficially practice on the road. If nothing else, your regular passengers sure will appreciate it!

Corner entry

Although we should always aim to exit the corners as fast as possible, this emphasis on the corner exit does not mean you can be slow into the corners. Obviously you need to brake as late as possible as this effectively makes the preceding straight longer, and you need to carry as much speed as you can into the corners to maintain momentum; speed, once lost, is not easily regained. But this should always be tempered by the need to exit the corners on the right line and with the maximum acceleration. If you leave your braking too late you will probably miss the turn-in point, and if you carry too much speed into the corner you will find it difficult to hold the car on line. Indeed, although the corner exit is critical, much of what happens at the exit is decided on corner entry.

You need to turn in at *exactly* the right place and at the right speed and turn the wheel the precise amount needed to clip the apex without having to make continual small adjustments to your line. If you achieve all of those things, the exit will pretty much take care of itself.

So, how do you decide how much you need to slow down going into a corner in order to obtain maximum acceleration out of it? Sorry, I can't answer that. There are no fixed rules; every corner is different and every car is different. The best drivers seem to have an intuition or feel for this; they can sense the optimum trade-off between cornering and acceleration, and hence the optimum line, within a few laps. For the rest of us it is probably a mixture of practice, repetition, experience and trial-and-error, which will allow us eventually to establish the right line on any given corner. Even then the line may vary minutely with every lap as it is extremely difficult to be totally consistent, and the faster you go the more difficult it becomes to do precisely the same thing lap after lap. You will always be making minor compensations or corrections for turning in a fraction too soon or too late, too sharply or not sharply

enough, pressing the throttle too early or too hard, and so on. That is why driving a car fast, thankfully, will always be an art.

Factors affecting cornering technique

Among the things we have to consider are the power and grip available. A very powerful car, for example, will demand more of a point-and-squirt technique to minimize wheelspin on corner exit. This means making a relatively slow corner entry and a tight early turn, then a long shallow exit, straightening the steering as early as possible to gain the maximum traction available for acceleration. Contrast that with the case of a car with more roadholding ability than power, which demands that you must maintain momentum by carrying a lot more speed into the corner and taking a line much nearer to that of a constant radius. Therefore the optimum line through any given corner will vary subtly depending on the performance characteristics of the car.

Gradient will also have an influence. The car will have more traction for acceleration on a downhill slope, but the traction available for braking will be less. Obviously the reverse also applies; on an uphill slope the wheels will spin more readily under hard acceleration but braking will be considerably improved. Any car will have more cornering traction and grip on an uphill turn than on a downhill one so we can take a line much nearer that of constant radius, whereas on a downhill turn we need to take a later apex because of the reduced grip. This becomes even trickier when you encounter a turn that is both uphill *and* downhill, *ie* with a pronounced dip or crest in the middle of it. If the corner entry is uphill, for example, the car will feel as though it has plenty of grip, but then it suddenly goes light on the crest, loses grip and slides wide on the exit. Obviously the opposite happens on a corner that starts downhill and exits uphill: you will seemingly have loads of traction coming out so you can take a much earlier apex.

Another important factor is the radius of the bend and hence the speed you can

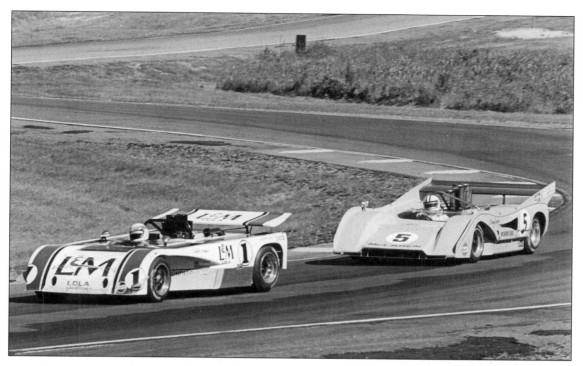

Immensely powerful cars like this Lola T260 and McLaren M8F, as raced in the legendary CanAm series, demand more of a point-and-squirt technique, where the line and corner entry speed must be compromised to allow the most traction for maximum acceleration.

Pronounced crests, like The Mountain at Cadwell Park, or Dingle Dell at Brands Hatch, may cause some or all of the wheels to lift off the ground momentarily at speed. The driver may have to feather the throttle to avoid over-revving the engine, and to prevent wheelspin on touch-down.

negotiate it. The faster the bend the nearer you can get to the line of maximum constant radius, *ie* the less of a late apex you need to make. If for example a car can achieve 120mph at the fastest part of the circuit (the majority of road cars probably get to within about 90% of their top speed on most circuits), if you can take a bend at, say, 100mph there is not much acceleration left before the vehicle reaches its terminal velocity for that particular circuit. The danger of spinning the wheels will be nil, and furthermore there will be much less weight transfer to the rear under acceleration. As we are trading off some of the tyres' cornering force in order for them to generate some traction to accelerate the car, if there is not much more acceleration to come, clearly less of a trade off is required, whereas if you are taking a

hairpin at, say, 40mph or less there is plenty of accelerating still to be done so we need to take a very late apex. Indeed, if you were able to take a bend at top speed there would be no acceleration left in the car, in which case the optimum line would probably be the geometrically perfect one.

A similar situation occurs when you have a fast bend closely followed by a much slower one, so you are forced to start braking more or less immediately after you exit the faster bend. If you are prevented from accelerating out of the bend you might as well carry as much speed as you can through it, which means using all the available tyre grip for cornering and taking the line of maximum constant radius. However, it is probably as well not to analyse this too much, but instead try to develop a *feel* for what the car and more

On an S-bend, the line is compromised to allow the greatest possible acceleration on to the straight that follows. That may mean holding a tight line through the first part of the corner, in order to allow the optimum line through the second.

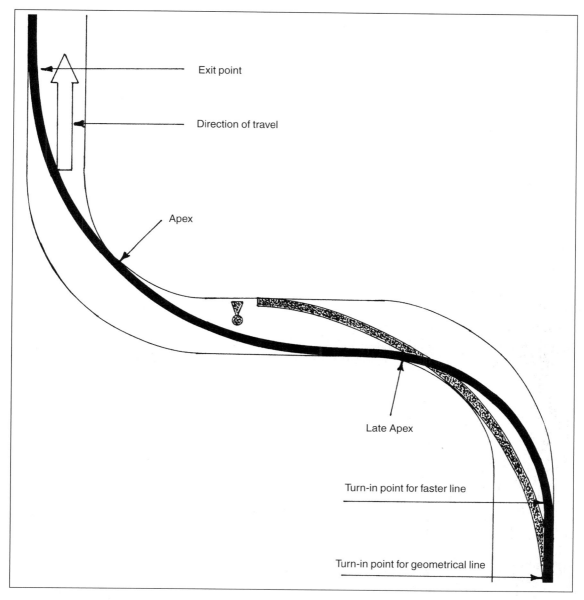

Exit point

Direction of travel

Apex

Late Apex

Turn-in point for faster line

Turn-in point for geometrical line

Illustration 11: Complex corner
When you have a sequence of one corner closely followed by another, it may be necessary to sacrifice some speed through the first corner in order to follow the optimum line through the second. In our example, note how taking the optimum line through the left-hander makes it impossible to get back on course to take the optimum line for the right-hander that follows. Assuming the right-hander leads onto a straight (or full-throttle section) then the line through the left-hander should be sacrificed in order to achieve maximum acceleration through the right-hander, and hence speed along the straight. Note the extremely late apex for the left-hander. Although the turn-in point is only slightly later, speed must be considerably less to allow for the much tighter turn demanded.

especially the tyres are doing. The good drivers seem to be able to do this intuitively, whereas some seem destined never to learn.

There is one circumstance, though, where a thoughtful and intelligent approach, rather than a purely instinctive one, may pay dividends, namely when you have two corners in very close proximity, so your line through one may be compromised by the need to take the optimum line through the other. From all of the foregoing you should be able to deduce that the corner to concentrate on is the one leading

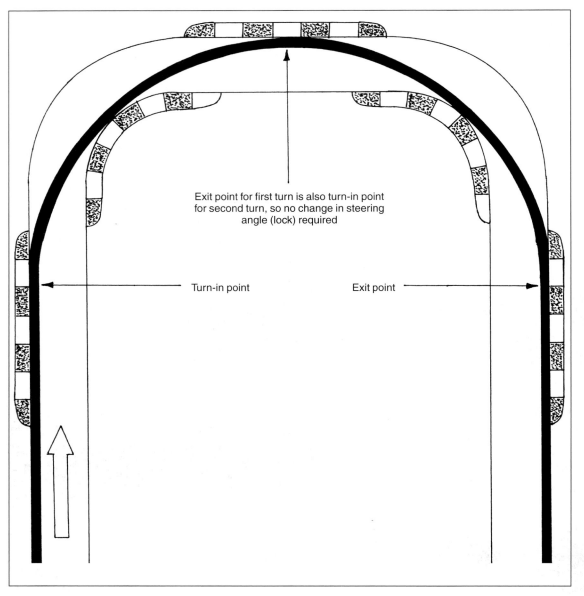

Exit point for first turn is also turn-in point
for second turn, so no change in steering
angle (lock) required

Turn-in point

Exit point

Illustration 12: Double-apex corner
Whenever possible, a double-apex corner should be driven as though it was a single corner, using as smooth an arc as possible to connect the two apexes. Your aim should be to keep steering movements to a minimum throughout. However, nature – and circuit designers! – seldom provide us with the perfect symmetry of our diagram. Be prepared to vary your line to allow for gradients, surface changes and lack of symmetry . . . and to allow maximum acceleration out of the corner, of course.

onto the straight – usually, but not necessarily, the last in the sequence. Let us assume you have a left-hander closely followed by a right-hander leading onto a straight (*Illustration 11*). Normally you would use the full road width exiting the left-hander, sweeping you out to the right-hand side of the track. But that would put you on the wrong line for the right-hander, for which obviously you need to be on the left-hand side. In that case you would sacrifice a little speed through the left-hander by braking more than you would otherwise need to and taking a very late apex. This will allow you to exit on the left-hand side, perfectly positioned to take the best line through the right-hander onto the straight at the best exit speed.

Two corners in quick succession in the same direction *(Illustration 12)* are usually referred to as a double-apex bend, which you should treat as one corner and try to negotiate in one smooth arc, although this may not always be possible. All the time you should be thinking about where you need to sacrifice a little speed in order to make a bigger gain elsewhere. This leads to the concept of prioritizing corners in their order of importance to your lap times. Having come this far you will no doubt realize that the most important corner on any circuit is the one leading onto the longest full-throttle section. Often this is not especially difficult, but if there is any conflict or compromise to be made, this is where it is important to make the right choices.

Rating the corners
You can then rate the remaining corners in order of importance. Of course, that doesn't mean you can be lazy or complacent on the corners that you reckon are of lesser importance. You still need to take them as fast as you can, maintaining the right balance between momentum and acceleration. To paraphrase George Orwell: all corners are important, but some are more important than others.

Eventually, given sufficient commitment and concentration, the optimum line through each corner, and in due course the entire circuit, will begin to emerge. Luckily, on track days you can concentrate purely on taking the optimum line all around the circuit, whereas when you are racing it is sometimes necessary to deviate from the ideal line so as not to make yourself vulnerable to being overtaken. Learning a circuit is a tremendous challenge, and even when you have driven many laps and know the circuit intimately it is still a challenge to try to drive the perfect lap.

The most important corner on a circuit is the one leading into the longest full-throttle section, where every additional mph of exit speed will be carried forward for as long as your car is able to continue accelerating.

12

SMOOTHLY DOES IT

Smoothness is a crucial element in fast driving, as virtually every driving manual ever written will tell you. It is a mantra that is repeated over and over, yet there have been few explanations as to *why* it is so important.

From all that you have read so far it should now be apparent that when cornering at the limit of adhesion, the speed we have chosen (given that we are using all the road to make the corner radius as large as possible) dictates the centrifugal force generated, which in turn dictates the amount of weight transferred to the outside tyres. The tyres respond to this increase in load by generating more cornering force, but also by increasing their slip angle; provided we have judged the cornering speed accurately they will then be operating at the optimum slip angle, and hence at the limit of adhesion. This corresponds with the maximum cornering force the vehicle will generate and, as we have seen earlier, cornering force and centrifugal force are equal, so completing the circle if you like.

Smooth driving

When slip angle and load are delicately balanced, as they are at the limit of adhesion, that equilibrium is all too easily disturbed, and that is why it is so important to drive smoothly when cornering at or near the limit of adhesion. Any variation in speed, steering angle or load can very easily disturb that delicate balance, so the controls must be handled with the utmost care and sensitivity. Essentially, when we talk about smooth driving we mean controlling or managing the weight transfer that takes place under acceleration, cornering and braking, and this means avoiding any violent or excessively large movements likely to disturb that balance.

But there is another, less obvious reason why we should strive to drive smoothly and control the transfer of weight as best we can. As we have seen, the cornering force developed by the outside tyres is dependent on the amount of weight transferred. The more weight is transferred, the more cornering force; but the increase in cornering force is not proportional to the increase in weight. It is in fact somewhat less. But what about the inside tyres? Well, as weight is transferred onto the outside tyres, logically (as the overall vehicle weight remains the same), the weight on the inside tyres is reduced; therefore the cornering force of the inside tyres is reduced. The crucial point is that the outside tyres don't gain as much as the inside tyres lose, and therefore overall cornering force is reduced.

This may be somewhat academic, as clearly we cannot limit weight transfer, much less avoid it altogether, as the limit of adhesion is virtually *defined* by the amount of weight transfer that takes place. But nevertheless in order to maintain maximum cornering force we should always try to keep weight transfer to a minimum so as to keep the inside tyres working as hard as possible. So on a corner that you can easily take flat you should always use all of the road width to make the corner radius as large as possible, even when you don't need to. You will transfer less weight, hence the inside tyres will be taking a greater share of the load; hence your tyre slip angles will be less; hence the tyres will generate less drag; hence you will go faster. You may also find that more of the tyres' potential is available for acceleration . . . but more on this later.

Conventional wisdom

Knowing *why* we should strive to drive smoothly is all very well, but *how* do we drive smoothly? The conventional wisdom, as found in some of the older driving manuals, suggests that you should always brake in a straight line, aim for a late apex by making a tight turn, then accelerate as hard as the tyres will allow in a straight or nearly straight line. In the old days, when race cars had no downforce and very little tyre grip, that was undoubtedly the case; what precious little grip there was had to be very carefully rationed between braking, cornering and acceleration. If the driver were to begin to turn while still braking, the competing demands on the tyres of braking and cornering at the same time would very easily exceed the tyres' limit of adhesion. Similarly if the driver tried to accelerate too hard or too soon coming out of a corner the tyres would spin all too readily, and a tyre that is spinning is not able to provide any cornering force.

Therefore the sporting motorist of old was advised to separate the three functions: braking, cornering and acceleration. Although that advice was generally sound, obviously if you do get all your braking done before attempting to turn into a corner there will be a period – however brief – during which the tyre, in making the transition, is not working hard. Indeed, Sir Stirling Moss reckons that one of the advantages he had over his contemporaries was his ability to brake right into the corners . . . but then he was probably one of the most skilled drivers ever, and perhaps possessed the balance and co-ordination that allowed him to do things others couldn't.

Whatever, times have changed. The advances in motor vehicle technology witnessed over a century or so of development have been nigh on miraculous, but perhaps the most remarkable progress has been in the field of tyres. As intimated earlier, the average road car driver today has more grip available from conventional road tyres than a Grand Prix driver of the 'fifties and early 'sixties (before the advent of unfeasibly wide 'slick' racing tyres). In motor racing, the advent of aerodynamic aids to artificially press the tyres harder onto the road surface (without any increase in weight) have led to ever-higher cornering speeds. In the process they also happen to have destroyed racing as a spectacle, but that's another story!

Even high-performance road tyres, though, offer so much grip that it is nowadays possible for even the moderately skilled driver to trade cornering force for braking traction or acceleration traction, and so ensure that he is getting the maximum grip from the tyres at all times. This means that as much as is practicable you should try to blend the three elements – accelerating, braking and cornering – into one smooth and seamless operation. Easy to say – or write! – but not quite so easy to achieve.

As you approach the turn-in point for a corner you should be easing pressure on the brake pedal, so the commencement of turning and the end of braking overlap. As you turn in, you should turn the wheel smoothly and progressively, not just wrench it over. This allows the tyres a little time to get used to the load you are putting on them . . . to take the strain, if you like, as weight transfer takes effect. You should apply the lock you need – no more, no less – to take you to the apex in one smooth, controlled motion, then smoothly and progressively feed off the lock as you accelerate, increasing throttle angle as you reduce steering angle and so freeing up the car for maximum acceleration as early as possible. If you like it may help to think of the steering wheel and pedals being connected so that the more steering you are doing the less you are able to do with the pedals. In the process you will be managing the progressive transfer of weight from the front tyres, which will be the more heavily loaded as you brake up to and perhaps just beyond the turn-in point, towards the rear tyres as you start to accelerate and gradually open out the corner.

A similar thing occurs under braking, when the nose of the car dips under the influence of forward weight transfer. The object of smooth braking then is to control forward weight transfer as best we can. Just as important is to *release* the brakes smoothly. When turning into a corner, ideally you should start to turn the wheel at the same time as you are easing up on the brakes, so these actions overlap and blend as much as is practicable. The importance of smoothness cannot be over-emphasized.

Oversteer and understeer

This is especially applicable when the track is wet, when the vehicle's fundamental handling characteristics may become exaggerated, and it slides more than it will on a dry track. Without going into too much complex discussion, the car is said to be understeering when the front tyres have a greater slip angle than the rears, while oversteer, logically enough, is the opposite, when the rear tyres have a greater slip angle than the fronts. Provided the car is cornering in a stable attitude, with only a modest difference between the front and rear slip angles, this causes few problems. Indeed, it is unusual to find a car with perfectly neutral steer characteristics at all speeds; usually the tyres at one end of the car will be operating at or perhaps slightly beyond the optimum slip angle and at the other end slightly below it. For example, if the front tyres are working at the optimum slip angle and the rears at a slightly lower slip angle the car will adopt a stable understeering attitude. Clearly the closer we can get to cornering with the same slip angles front and rear the better as a car with perfectly balanced handling will be easier to drive quickly, and faster too.

Sliding

Problems arise, however, when there is a large difference between the front and rear slip angles such that the tyres at one end exceed their optimum slip angle when those at the other end are still some way from doing so, causing the tyres at one end to slide. An understeering car feels as though it is not responding to the steering properly and will tend to run wide in the corner, or will demand more steering lock to maintain the chosen line. This is often accompanied by the steering feeling strange: it may either feel heavy and 'dead' or vague and light. When the car oversteers the rear tyres slide, causing the tail of the car to slide out in the corners in extreme cases. An oversteering car will continue to tighten its line through the corner, and if not corrected this will usually result in a spin. This may be avoided by steering into the slide, *ie* away from the corner; in other words, applying opposite lock.

An important distinction between oversteer and understeer is that understeer can be described as self-correcting, whereas oversteer demands positive and correct action from the driver. When the front tyres are sliding (*ie* the car is understeering) excessively, drag is created, which rapidly slows the car to the point where the front tyres regain grip and steering control is restored, even when the driver does nothing. With any luck, provided the car has not run so wide as to leave the road, it will still be pointing vaguely in the right direction and the driver can simply gather his wits and proceed. However, an oversteering car, if left to its own devices with no input from the driver, will soon spin out of control. Just like the understeering car, because of tyre drag it will slow down and eventually come to a halt, but where is anyone's guess. That is why manufacturers usually prefer to design their passenger cars with some built-in understeer, as it is justifiably considered safer for the average driver.

As a very broad generalization front-wheel-drive cars tend to understeer and rear-wheel-drive cars tend to oversteer.

Whether a car understeers or oversteers in steady-state cornering is inherent in the design and layout and depends on the tyre characteristics, static weight distribution and weight transfer in cornering (the dynamic weight distribution, in other words). You may rightly deduce from this that weight is the crucial element.

We have learnt that the more weight on a tyre the more grip it will produce, although the increase in weight is not matched by a commensurate increase in cornering force; the relationship is not linear and therefore grip is finite. It should be apparent then that the way the weight is distributed between the four tyres, and the way it moves between them during braking, cornering and acceleration (ignoring, for simplicity's sake, the effect of camber change and other effects of suspension movement) largely dictates whether the car will oversteer or understeer in steady-state cornering.

In reality, though, steady-state cornering – which implies that the car is cornering on a constant radius, a level gradient and a smooth surface and is neither accelerating nor slowing down – doesn't exist. Even in the rare event that most of those elements are in place the driver will usually be trying to accelerate, and therefore what he does with the brake and accelerator pedals and the steering wheel have a major influence on the handling of the car. Severe understeer or oversteer are often the result of clumsy or inept driver inputs.

In that case the real problem is one of driver technique, not vehicle dynamics. Largely, therefore, skilled driving is a matter of managing the weight transfer that occurs as a result of braking, accelerating and cornering, recognizing and allowing for the vehicle's limitations and getting the best from the tyres. To maintain the optimum tyre slip angles while cornering, braking, and accelerating takes considerable skill and sensitivity. Throw in the effect of bumps in the road, gradient, camber, changes in road surface, track temperature, etc, and you can see that this requires considerable expertise. Although cars, and particularly tyres, are now infinitely better than those of old, driving fast is thankfully still as demanding and difficult as ever. After all, if it was easy it wouldn't be anything like as much fun, would it?

One of the many skills we need to acquire is accurate steering, which is the subject of the next chapter, *Steering Techniques*.

Whether a car understeers or oversteers in steady-state cornering is determined by its static weight distribution and its tyres' characteristics; the art of skilful driving is controlling weight transfer (dynamic weight distribution) so as to achieve maximum tyre performance.

13

STEERING TECHNIQUES

A willingness to learn is essential if you wish to become a smoother, faster, safer driver. As you gain track day experience you will inevitably become more competent, and this will in turn give you the confidence to go faster. As your speed increases it should be obvious that precise and accurate steering is vital.

Making the connection

In order to steer accurately at high speed you need to know *exactly* where the front wheels are aimed at all times, and the best way to do that – the *only* way in my view – is to always keep your hands in the same place on the wheel, fixing them in the most comfortable position and keeping them there as much as practicable, certainly at anything above town driving speeds. This allows you to relate the position of your hands to the angle of the front wheels, and very quickly becomes instinctive so that you don't have to look at your hands or even think about it to know what the front wheels are doing. In time, you need only look to where you want to go and your hands will respond automatically, turning the wheel the required amount.

Doin' the shuffle

This may, however, be alien to many, especially those who have learnt to drive in the UK, and who have been taught to feed the steering wheel through their hands in the infamous 'BSM shuffle'. When this

technique was evolved in the 1920s it addressed many of the problems faced by drivers in those days. At that time, steering wheels were huge – perhaps 18 to 20 inches in diameter – and they had to be because steering systems in common use at that time were ponderous, slow and heavy, and the driver needed to be able to apply plenty of leverage. At the same time the steering in most vehicles was low-geared, so drivers needed to turn the wheel a long way to get a little lock; perhaps as much as a quarter-turn was used just taking up the slack! The road wheels were also large and heavy, and because they were carried on live axles with primitive kingpins, steering shimmy (gyroscopic precession) was an ever-present hazard. At higher speeds this could at times be severe enough to tear the wheel from the driver's hands, so a firm grip was essential.

Bearing in mind the very different demands of the day, the BSM shuffle was probably a perfectly valid technique . . . at the time. But things have changed. Sporting motorists nowadays enjoy the benefits of light and direct steering, power-assisted in most cases. As a result, steering wheels today are typically around 13 or 14 inches in diameter, or even smaller in the case of many sports cars. Many cars have wide, low-profile tyres offering vastly greater grip, so cornering speeds have increased enormously. Cars are generally much lower, and we tend to adopt a much

The infamous BSM shuffle was a method of steering evolved for vehicles like this; slow and often heavy steering demanded plenty of leverage, provided by a large and upright steering wheel, which required a firm grip. It has no place in the modern motor vehicle, and it definitely has no place on the race track.

more reclined and relaxed seat position, semi-recumbent in some sports cars. Road surfaces have improved (a generalization with which some will doubtless take exception!) and, thanks to a century of development and with the benefit of sophisticated computer-aided design techniques, steering and suspension design have also advanced enormously, so steering kickback and bump steer are much less common than they were (although sadly they have not been eradicated altogether). Therefore, I believe the BSM shuffle to be no longer appropriate for modern cars and modern driving conditions, and it most *certainly* has no place on a race circuit.

You will be hard pressed to find any serious competition driver who advocates feeding the wheel, which should tell you something. Even rally drivers, who often need to use more of the available lock as they routinely get into the most extravagant slides, will usually keep their chosen grip on the wheel if they can. For those moments when they do need to use more lock they often have a strip of tape on

the top of the steering wheel so they can easily establish the straight-ahead position when twirling the wheel. This simply reinforces the point that in order to maintain full control at high speed you need to know where the front wheels are aimed.

Sadly, though, the BSM shuffle is still the officially approved method, as those responsible for testing new drivers remain in a time warp, which is probably why you see so many learner drivers making such unfeasibly hard work of steering the car, gripping the wheel as though they have got hold of the business end of a highly poisonous snake, terrified to let go. Most of us at some time will have seen some hapless learner driver veering towards the kerb after rounding a bend (perhaps we have even *been* that hapless learner!) simply through not having wound off the lock quickly enough, yet they are discouraged from allowing the steering to self-centre. But provided you allow the wheel to slip through your hands under control there is no earthly reason in my opinion why you cannot use the vehicle's self-centring action – which the designers have so kindly provided for you – to return to the straight-ahead position.

Police warning

Suggest this to a trained police driver, though, and he will probably have a fit. For many years the police have been the stoutest advocates of what they call the push-pull method of steering, the BSM shuffle in other words. The police have long considered themselves the foremost, if not the only, experts on driving technique (ignoring all the evidence to the contrary!) and in particular they have ignored, and indeed scorned, the expertise and experience of competition drivers who have long since abandoned the shuffle.

Ironically, *Roadcraft*, the official police driver's handbook, which was first published in the 1930s, was written in consultation with Sir Malcolm Campbell and Lord Cottenham, two of the leading racing drivers of the day, and therefore reflected the accepted best practice at that time. There are encouraging signs, though, that at last the police have woken up to the fact that vehicles have changed somewhat since then, and therefore driving techniques have changed too. The latest edition of *Roadcraft* recognizes what they refer to as rotational steering (which is not a bad description come to think of it!), and acknowledges that it may be appropriate 'during skidding or during very slow or high speed manoeuvres'. Which is what I have argued all along . . .

There was a time when I would have argued that it was *impossible* to control a sliding car properly using the shuffle until I rode with a former police driving instructor on a skidpan, who demonstrated the most amazing car control while moving his hands no more than about 10cm (5cm each way) from his static hand position, shuffling the wheel at great speed but with unerring accuracy, his hands a blur. It may have looked awkward but it was certainly effective, and therefore I would never argue that it was impossible; but I still maintain it is bloody difficult! Our skidpan maestro had evidently honed his skills over many

years and he was indisputably brilliant, but even *he* couldn't make it look easy.

I still believe that for high-speed driving the shuffle is fundamentally flawed. When you need to get lock on or off in a hurry it's simply not fast enough, and when you need real precision it's not accurate enough. Sadly, perhaps, you must still master the BSM shuffle in order to pass your driving test, but at least once you have done so you can bin it and revert to a much more natural and efficient style of steering. However, this does not mean that I am advocating that you should never under any circumstances feed the wheel through your hands in the approved manner. I accept that there are many occasions when this is preferable, or even unavoidable: when parking, for example, or when manoeuvring in the pits or paddock, or when negotiating tight turns at very slow town driving speeds.

But here we are concerned with driving at speed on a circuit, when I maintain that steering with both hands fixed on the wheel is more relaxed and natural, is more accurate – which promotes a smoother and more flowing driving style – and is faster. Of course, there are those diehards who disagree, and therefore what you should aim for above all is whatever feels the most natural technique for you, so if feeding the wheel through your hands is so deeply ingrained in your psyche and your driving style that you simply cannot change, don't worry too much about this – just carry on with what you find the most comfortable. After all, at high speed through the faster corners, where steering accuracy is the most critical, you don't so much steer the car as aim it, and because the amount of lock you need to apply is so small you will probably not feel the need to shuffle anyway, while on the slower corners it is arguably not quite as critical.

Cross your arms

Those who preach the shuffle dogma argue that your hands should never pass through the 12 o'clock position, as though the wheel were divided vertically into left and right zones and your hands should never stray from their allotted zone. But assuming your

Contrary to dogma preached in certain circles, crossing the arms in a tight corner is not fatal, nor even slightly painful! If you feed the wheel through your hands you will not be able to steer as accurately, but perhaps more importantly you will not be able to return quickly and accurately to the straight-ahead position.

chosen hand position is quarter-to-three, you can safely cross your arms to rotate the wheel until your hands are reversed, *ie* the left hand has gone to 3 o'clock and the right has assumed the quarter-to (9 o'clock) position. This allows you to steer a half-turn in each direction, giving you a full turn of lock altogether, and provided you are driving something at least moderately sporty, this will supply enough steering angle on even the tightest hairpin or chicane at most circuits.

Purpose-built race cars have very fast steering and usually very limited lock, so the drivers can keep their hands firmly fixed on the wheel even in the tightest hairpin bends. Of course, road cars necessarily have slower steering than race cars and more lock is available in order to provide a reasonable turning circle, so if your car's steering is not *quite* quick enough and you need more lock than you can achieve with crossed arms, by all means reposition one hand to gain a little more leverage, but it is always advisable to keep the other one in the 'correct' position if

possible to serve as a datum point for when you return to the straight-ahead position.

Self-centring

Occasionally, though, you may need to use more lock than usual, requiring you to feed the wheel, such as when correcting a slide or skid, especially when you have been caught out by an unexpectedly slippery surface. In those cases, allowing the steering to self-centre may well be the quickest and most accurate method of returning the wheel to the straight-ahead position. However, you must keep it under control at all times, allowing the rim to slide back through your hands; never release your grip entirely. As I have said in *Smoothly Does It*, this is most likely to occur on a wet track, when the car's fundamental handling characteristics tend to become exaggerated, causing it to slide much more than in the dry.

Corrective measures

It should be obvious that when the car does slide you need to take corrective measures,

Front-wheel drive has many disadvantages on the circuit. Nevertheless, this Honda Integra-R makes light of all those disadvantages and is devastatingly fast on the circuit in the right hands.

steering in the appropriate direction rapidly and accurately. If the front wheels slide it is because you have exceeded the optimum slip angle of the tyres. In order to regain control you need to reduce the centrifugal force acting on the vehicle, so the weight transferred to the outside tyres – or more specifically the outside front tyre – is reduced. Remembering the factors that influence centrifugal force, you can do this either by slowing down or increasing the cornering radius. If we try to brake, however, this will increase weight transfer onto the front wheels, which is likely to make the problem worse. You should therefore avoid braking and limit any attempt to slow down to easing smoothly off the throttle.

But if you can reduce steering lock (*ie* increase the corner radius) it will reduce the tyre slip angle *and* the lateral weight transfer, both of which should help to restore grip to the outside front tyre. However, your natural reaction when the vehicle is not responding to your steering inputs in the way you expect is to crank on more lock, so it may take considerable presence of mind to reduce the lock (*and* avoid braking!) in order to regain control. Of course, by doing so you make a wider turn, which introduces the possibility of

running off the road altogether before you have regained control – clearly a situation best avoided!

If you use a front-wheel-drive car at track days you may find you have inadvertently induced understeer by applying the throttle when the tyres are still fully occupied providing maximum cornering force. Obviously the solution in that case is to ease off the throttle, although again you should do this as smoothly as possible; don't lift off suddenly.

When the rear tyres of a rear-wheel-drive car slide it is usually because you have applied the throttle too enthusiastically and exceeded the rear tyres' total tractive capability. To maintain control you need to steer into the slide by reducing the steering lock and perhaps even applying a little opposite lock. This effectively increases the corner radius, so reducing centrifugal force; at the same time the reduction in slip angle reduces the cornering force generated by the front tyres, helping to restore balance to the distribution of cornering force front-to-rear. Logically you should also reduce power to the rear wheels to allow the rear tyres to recover some cornering force. If you lift off the throttle abruptly, though, there is a danger that the sudden restoration of cornering force to the rear will further unsettle the car, especially when you are steering away from the inside of the corner. The danger then is that the car will snap the other way, which will almost invariably result in a loss of control, so it is even more imperative that you ease off the throttle smoothly and with great finesse.

In practice what you usually do is a little of both – steer into the slide and ease off the throttle, albeit not altogether. However, it is very difficult to co-ordinate these actions smoothly, to ease off the throttle just the right amount and apply just the right amount of opposite lock to drive smoothly out of the slide. Bear in mind also that when you apply opposite lock you are steering away from the inside of the corner, effectively making the corner radius larger, so there is a danger that this may lead you to run out of road before the corner exit. One tip that may prove useful is to focus your eyes on where you want to go, and provided you have established that crucial correlation between your hand positioning on the steering wheel and the front wheels of the car, as I have suggested, you should be able to rely on your hands to steer you in the right direction. But in reality it is impossible to advise or teach anyone how much to ease off the throttle, or how much opposite lock to apply. The only way to learn is to practice ... practice ... practice; but even if you do it may be a long time before you develop truly outstanding car control, which may well be a talent (you've either got it or you haven't!) rather than a skill (that you can acquire).

Catching the slide

Obviously you need to steer quickly and accurately when correcting a slide, but when you have 'caught' the slide – in other words when grip has been restored to the tyres – you need to be every bit as quick and accurate in taking off the corrective lock. When you steer to correct a slide, sooner or later the sliding tyres will regain their grip and the car will respond normally to the steering and go wherever the front wheels are pointing. Consequently, if you have a lot of lock applied to counter severe understeer, when the front tyres regain

their grip the car will very abruptly steer towards the inside of the corner, which can cause a nasty surprise, especially if the corner is lined with Armco or, even more exciting, a concrete retaining wall! Hence my advice to reduce steering lock if you can when you encounter understeer, however unnatural this may seem. As I mentioned in *Tyre Performance*, you need to develop a feel for the tyres, which is a matter of practice and experience. You cannot expect to acquire this overnight.

Similarly, when you apply opposite lock to counteract oversteer, when the rear tyres regain their bite the car will go wherever the front wheels are pointing, in this case towards the outside of the corner. This explains why you occasionally see cars spin off in the 'wrong' direction, *ie* on a right-hand bend they spin off to the left. This is often referred to as over-correcting, the implication being that you have applied too much opposite lock, whereas in fact the cause is more likely to be that you were a little too slow in *removing* the opposite lock when the tyres have suddenly regained their grip, because you failed to recognize that the grip was about to be restored.

An interesting variation of this phenomenon is sometimes referred to as a 'tankslapper' (which is actually a bit of motorcycle jargon hijacked by the four-wheeled brigade). This occurs when the tyres suddenly regain grip and you don't *quite* get the opposite lock off in time, but just manage to prevent the car from spinning the wrong way by steering rapidly in the opposite direction. Once you have gotten 'behind' the car, though, it is very difficult to catch up and you need a lot of skill and some luck in order to regain control, not least because in using lots of steering lock you can very quickly lose track of where the front wheels are pointing. Then you usually end up frantically steering one way then the other as the car 'fishtails' up the road in a series of wild swerves until you finally end up spinning about 200 yards from where you first 'lost it'!

Indeed, if you recognize early on that you are getting into a tankslapper you may be better off letting the car spin rather than

When you get really sideways, like this, it is vitally important to react quickly to apply the right amount of corrective lock; just as important is to recognize when grip is about to be restored, and to return quickly and accurately to the straight-ahead position when it is.

trying to fight it because the swerves often become ever more pronounced. If you surrender peacefully and allow the car to spin early in the sequence you might retain some semblance of control and spin harmlessly to a halt, whereas if you fight and lose you will probably end up spinning violently, perhaps at greater speed, with unpredictable results. This may mean the difference between a harmless spin and a sudden impact with something hard and unyielding! However, it takes some experience to recognize when to fight to retain control and when to give in gracefully.

Clearly, then, in order to control a slide you need to be able to sense when the tyres have lost grip, but it is just as important to be able to sense when they are about to regain it. There are those brilliant instinctive drivers – the 'naturals' – who seem to have a feel for the tyres' limit of adhesion and are able to handle a car at and sometimes even over the limit with ease. Whereas most of us react to what the car is doing – with varying degrees of success! – the naturals seem to have a total rapport with the car, controlling and correcting slides before they have even happened. Few beginners have this skill, and some drivers *never* acquire it.

For evidence of this you need only watch *Top Gear*, or one of the other motoring programmes on television, as one of the show's presenters slides a car about for the cameras. Note how it is relatively easy to put the car into a slide, but not so easy to pull it *out* of one gracefully; often the car will give a little wriggle before it is completely straight, or rock on its suspension because it has been pulled back into line clumsily. To be fair to the presenters, in order to make it look spectacular for the cameras they are often required to get the car into a *big* slide, which is much more difficult to control than a small one, primarily because correcting it requires you to use more lock than you can apply by crossing your arms. It is very easy to get lost when twirling the wheel, and finding your way smoothly back to the straight-ahead position requires good reactions and considerable sensitivity and skill.

Bearing in mind that the drivers we see on television motoring programmes are extremely competent in the main, it is apparent that *real* finesse is rare. The majority of us can only ever aspire to competence. As I have said, practice is the key, and there is no substitute for what Americans call 'seat time'. Certainly while you are still learning, and gaining the experience you need to be able to feel what the car is doing or is about to do, it is advisable to avoid sliding it about excessively and, if caught by surprise, try to catch a slide before it gets too big. It is probably rare for a reasonably competent driver to lose control when using what the police call rotational steering, but it is easy for even a skilled driver to lose it once he has used more than half-a-turn of lock in either direction and is having to 'twirl' the wheel.

Although you may think it is more spectacular and more fun to throw the car about in lurid slides, as we have seen in *Tyre Performance,* the tyres do not generate as much grip when they are sliding as when they are at the limit of adhesion. It is one of the curious ironies of motorsport that the most spectacular driving is the least effective. It is more hazardous – for the novice anyway – *and* it is usually slower.

There is a popular image of race drivers, perpetuated in a string of b-movies and crap television programs, which suggests that racing, or indeed any form of fast driving, involves lots of gritted teeth and furious sawing at the wheel. That is because the directors seem to believe that in order to look fast, race drivers need to be really busy with the steering. Watch the aces in action, though, and you will see that the very opposite is the case. The best of the best make it look so easy because in fact they steer very little. Which, it must be admitted, probably doesn't make for very exciting movie or television action for those who don't know any better.

Economy of steering

In fact, one of the key elements of fast driving is steering *as little as possible*. This concept, which seems so curious on the face of it, incorporates many of the principles I have touched on earlier. In the first instance it means choosing the right line through the corner. The right line is one that allows you to turn in smoothly, hold the right amount of lock throughout the bend and smoothly unwind the lock as the road straightens before you, without making any minute corrections that may disturb the tyres' tenuous hold on the road. If you steer too sharply when you turn in, for example, you will find you are about to clip the inside of the corner too early; this will cause you to steer away momentarily and, in all probability, tighten your line again beyond the apex. Conversely, if you don't turn enough you will miss the apex, then you will have to apply more lock as you approach the exit of the corner to avoid running out of road. These adjustments of line become critical when the load on the tyre and the slip angle are so delicately balanced that every tiny swerve can cause an increase in tyre slip angle or load, and so exceed the limit of adhesion.

The second aspect of steering as little as possible is to avoid sliding the car excessively and having to correct for excessive understeer or oversteer, causing you to wind on more lock or opposite lock, respectively, in order to maintain your chosen line. As stated earlier, some understeer or oversteer may be inherent in the car, but it is very much affected by driver input. Therefore you should drive within the limitations of the vehicle and make the necessary allowances. If you experience a lot of understeer or oversteer on corner entry you should think very carefully about braking distances and corner entry speeds. It may be better to brake earlier, enter the corner at slightly lower speed and accelerate progressively through it. On the other hand, if the car oversteers (or understeers) heavily under acceleration, this is often the result of imprudent or undisciplined use of the accelerator and you need to use it more progressively. Another alternative may be to try to carry more speed into the corner to achieve a better balance. All the time you should be thinking about how to help the car and co-operate with it, rather than fight it.

The third aspect to consider is keeping tyre slip angles, and hence tyre drag, to the very minimum, bearing in mind that the optimum slip angle will give you the most grip for the least drag. Even if the car is steering reasonably neutrally, remember that any time you are cornering with some steering lock applied the tyres are adopting a slip angle, and that means drag, which robs horsepower and costs speed. Clearly, therefore, the longer and more often you can keep the wheels straight the better. Obviously, because you need some slip angle in order to generate any cornering force you cannot avoid *some* tyre scrub, but remember that scrub is preventing you from obtaining maximum power and acceleration, so try to straighten the steering as soon as possible after every corner.

You could describe this as economy of steering. The right line through any given bend, therefore, will be the one that allows you to straighten the steering and apply maximum acceleration as early as possible, while making allowances as necessary for the handling characteristics of the car. You should try to obtain maximum acceleration with minimum steering. If possible, try to restrict your steering movements to what you can apply without removing your hands from the wheel. Again, this is why I emphasize the importance of establishing that crucial correlation between your hands and the front wheels of the car.

So far we have examined the importance of obtaining maximum acceleration out of every bend and how this affects the line we take through the corners and ultimately around the entire circuit. But there are obviously times when we also need to slow down, and that is the subject of *Braking Techniques*.

Economy of steering demonstrated by saloon car expert Andy Rouse as he heads for a late apex on a corner at Thruxton during another winning BTCC drive in his Sierra. The less steering movement you can make in achieving and holding on to the correct line, the faster you will be.

14

BRAKING TECHNIQUES

For a number of reasons I would counsel against most track day drivers exploring the outer reaches of the brake envelope. The first is that it is not terribly productive. You only spend a relatively small proportion of each lap – usually less than 10% – slowing down, so any improvement you can make through better braking technique has only a moderate effect on your lap times: you are much better off concentrating on the remaining 90% of the lap.

As an example, let us assume you are lapping a circuit in 1min 40sec, or 100 seconds. This means you will only be braking for around 10 seconds or less. Clearly, in order to improve your lap time by just a second you would need to make a 10% improvement in braking performance. In reality you will probably find this fairly difficult to do, assuming you are already trying moderately hard in the braking areas. Indeed, the difference between trying moderately hard and leaving a reasonable margin for error, as you should do on a track day, and trying bloody hard with *no* margin for error, as you do when racing, is mainly in how hard and how late you brake. It is probably only worth about a 1% improvement in lap times, perhaps a little more. Whatever, unless you are in a competitive situation there is no point in pushing for those last few fractions of a second, especially when you are not supposed to be timing laps in any case!

Penalty of failure
The second reason to exercise restraint in the braking zone is that mistakes can be costly. If you err on the side of caution and brake a little too early, or slow down a little more than you really need to . . . so what? Remember that too little speed is always preferable to too much! You might chide yourself for being a little slower than you could have been, but it's not as though you have lost a race as a result. When racing it may be easier to justify to yourself (and your wife or partner, the rest of the team, your sponsor . . . and perhaps your bank manager!) if you make a mistake and bend your motor in the pursuit of greater glory. It's a pity, of course, but sometimes that is the price of success. But there can be little excuse for bending your motor on a track day. After all, a track day is supposed to be non-competitive. You're there for fun and enjoyment.

If you are going to make an expensive mistake on the race track it will most likely be under braking, and it needn't be a big mistake either. Usually it will be the result of braking only fractionally too late, or perhaps too hard. A very minor error of judgment under braking can have major repercussions.

That is because a car will slow down very much more quickly than it will accelerate. The brakes are a good deal more powerful than the engine, not least because all of the forces that work against you

Because the brakes of most high-performance cars are nowadays so powerful, braking distances are short, leaving little margin for error. Consequently most mistakes occur in the braking areas, and for exactly the same reasons they are more likely to have serious repercussions. Best avoided.

under acceleration – friction, inertia, drag, etc – work *for* you under braking. The faster you go the more pronounced the effect becomes, largely because aerodynamic drag increases with the square of speed. This means that at 60mph aero drag is four times as great as at 30mph, while at 120mph it will be 16 times as great. This effect is felt most keenly when you ride a bicycle. Pedalling gently along at 10mph, the wind resistance can be felt as a gentle zephyr, but double your speed to 20mph and the wind resistance is enough to make pedalling much harder and to bring tears to your eyes. In your car, if you lift off the throttle at a steady 90mph, say, you will slow down much more quickly, initially at least, than when you lift off at a steady 45mph. This is why the rate of acceleration slows markedly the nearer we come to a vehicle's maximum speed and why the brakes seem even more effective the faster you go. All of which means that most cars will take three to five times as long to accelerate from rest to maximum speed as to brake from maximum speed to standstill.

Modern high-performance cars generally have excellent brakes, which, combined with the grip available from the latest tyres, offer very efficient retardation. That is great, of course, but it also means that braking distances are much shorter and therefore the margins for error are correspondingly less, which makes the driver's job more difficult. If you are a split second late getting back on the power coming out of a corner you might lose a little speed on the following straight, which may be frustrating, but nothing more. But if you brake a fraction too late you will arrive at some critical point on the circuit – usually a turn-in point for a bend – going too fast, which can very rapidly get you into difficulties. Because the braking areas are far more condensed a split second is much more critical, which is another argument in favour of leaving a little more margin for error.

Outbraking yourself
If you leave your braking too late, one of several things may happen. Usually you will realize more-or-less immediately that you have made a mess of things. You will then be tempted to press the brake pedal

even harder, in which case you will almost certainly lock the brakes. You then take longer still to slow down because, as we have seen in *Tyre Performance*, for maximum retardation the wheels should be kept rotating at around 5-15% slip. When you realize that you are not slowing down as quickly as you intended the natural reaction is to press the brake pedal even harder, so you can soon get into a vicious circle that is difficult to break. You need considerable presence of mind to *release* the brake pedal when panic is pounding in your chest and your every instinct is to press the pedal harder. Leaving aside the fact that by locking your brakes you can very quickly ruin your tyres, you will also lose any ability to steer, and if the circuit layout forces you to brake while turning, or if your braking system is not in the best condition, causing them to lock unevenly, you could even lose control altogether. Therefore, jamming the brakes on hard is just about the worst thing you can do.

Instead you must remain calm, brake just hard enough to keep the wheels from locking, and seek an escape route. Because braking distances nowadays are so short you rarely have much time or room to work with, so it can help if you have planned ahead. In other words, when you are learning the circuit and are still circulating slowly enough to take in the surrounding features you should be looking for potential escape routes and mentally filing them away.

When you realize you have outbraked yourself your top priority should be to abort the lap. By that I mean you must forget about making it a fast lap and taking the normal line through the approaching corner. Be prepared to sacrifice your line through the corner and your speed out of it; indeed, do *anything* just to keep you and the car away from the Armco. You're just trying to *survive,* dammit!

Assuming you arrive at the turn-in point going too fast and probably still hard on the brakes, if you attempt to turn in with the brakes locked you will just plough straight on, so all you can do is hope that you scrub off enough speed before you run out of tarmac . . . and luck! If you have

managed to keep the wheels rolling but you turn in going too fast or still braking hard, a spin is a virtual certainty. Depending on the circuit layout, your speed and the proximity of Armco, gravel traps, traffic and so on, this may be the best option, although it is likely to be risky, so you should look for a safer one. If you decide to turn in knowing you are still going too fast, make it a conscious decision; don't just turn in and hope for the best. This way you will be ready for the spin when it comes and may be able to keep it under some semblance of control . . . if that is not a contradiction in terms.

Stand on everything

If you get into a spin, for whatever reason, it is best to accept that your control of the situation is limited, if not lost altogether. Usually, once the tyres have lost their grip, the safest thing to do is to lock the brakes and spin to a halt as quickly as possible. Some drivers seem (or claim!) to be able to control a spinning car with judicious use of steering, brakes and throttle. This may be possible, but it is a risky stratagem because the only way to retain steering control is to let the brakes off to allow the wheels to rotate, which inevitably will prolong the spin.

More crucially it makes the spin much more unpredictable and erratic because whenever the tyres are not scrubbing sideways across the road and the wheels are free to roll the car will go wherever the wheels are pointing. That is why you often see cars suddenly shooting backwards when they have spun through 180 degrees, then spinning again in a random pattern. The problem is that if you 'fight' the spin it is all too easy to become disoriented and lose track of where you are, which way you are facing and where the front wheels are pointing. You need sharp wits, a lot of skill, nerves of steel and a bit of luck, too, to get away with this. Experience will help, but clearly there is no way of acquiring the required experience without some risk.

The safer option is usually just to jam the brakes on and get the car slowed sufficiently to allow you to regain control as quickly as you can. Okay, it won't do your tyres much good; you might end up with some fairly spectacular flat spots. If you do keep it out of the Armco, though (bearing in mind that there are no guarantees even if you *do* follow my advice and stand on the brakes), this will seem a small price to pay.

With the brakes locked a car will usually spin in a long lazy arc, rather than quickly and unpredictably. It is difficult to explain this rationally, but it seems to 'dampen' the spin somehow. If you can contrive to dip the clutch or flick the gear-lever into neutral you should be able to keep the engine going, although if you need to blip the throttle as well as pressing the brake pedal and dipping the clutch you may feel as though you need three feet (you do know how to heel-and-toe, don't you?). However, it is desirable to keep the engine running if you can; a stationary car straddling the circuit represents a hazard to other track users so it is essential that you move out of the way as quickly as possible, and a stalled engine will cost precious seconds.

Once the car has slowed almost to a halt you can assess the situation: Is the engine still running? Which gear are we in? Which direction are we facing? . . . prior to driving away, chastened perhaps, but hopefully with the car intact. It is vital to keep your wits about you. On many occasions I have seen drivers, disorientated after a spin, gently nudge the barriers or roll agonizingly slowly into the path of an oncoming vehicle simply because they haven't had the sense to press the brake pedal when the car is almost stationary and effectively back under control; they have damaged their cars, and sometimes other people's, quite unnecessarily. There is no excuse for this, which is another argument in favour of standing on the brakes as soon as you realize you are past the point of no return. The trick, needless to say, is to recognize the point of no return.

Great escape

Back, though, to the problem of what to do when you misjudge your braking. By far the best way to get yourself out of trouble is to use the escape road if there is one. You

If you do make a mistake and leave your braking too late, by far the best remedy is to use the escape road if available. This is where a little reconnaissance when learning the circuit can pay dividends later; learning and memorizing any potential escape routes can prepare you to deal with the problem when it occurs.

If you are fast, skilled . . . and lucky, you may be able to steer your way out of a spin. For most of us, though, the best solution is to lock the brakes, dip the clutch, and get it over with as rapidly as possible. "Spin? – both feet in" . . . but use your third foot to keep the engine running if possible.

can then ease off the brakes and bring the car to a halt in a calm and controlled manner. This is where having an awareness of your surroundings by doing a little reconnaissance while learning the circuit can prove invaluable.

Another option is to use the full width of the circuit to make the braking area as long as possible. You need to look for the longest and preferably straightest stretch of tarmac and use it to lose as much speed as possible in the space available, bearing in mind that the brakes are capable of slowing you very quickly provided you do not panic and lock them. However, you will not be able to brake as rapidly on grass – even less so if the grass is wet – and you may not be able to steer, so if you are still going too fast when you reach the limit of the tarmac you will rapidly run out of options. It requires fine judgment to decide

how much speed you can shed in the room you have available.

If you do run out of tarmac you may still get away with it *provided you have slowed sufficiently*. If you have watched motorsport, either live or on television, you will have seen how little grip there is on the grass, how drivers often lose control at what seem like comically low speeds and how often they struggle to regain the circuit, especially if the grass is wet or they have come to rest on even the gentlest slope. Compared to the grey stuff, the green stuff really is incredibly slippery.

If you do go off, therefore, you need to ensure there is little or no centrifugal force (cornering force) acting on the car which, as you should know by now, is a matter of going very slowly or making an extremely large corner radius. If you slide off out of control you're probably in trouble, the great danger in sliding across the grass at speed being that the car will 'dig in' and flip over. The grass run-off area is unlikely to be perfectly smooth, and it may take only the slightest imperfection – a soft patch of earth, perhaps, a drainage ditch, a decent-sized rock or even an animal burrow – to trip the car. If you take a high-speed excursion across the grass and emerge unscathed you really are riding your luck.

Patience

If you have the option, it may be preferable to deliberately drive off the circuit under control. By keeping the lateral 'g' to a minimum you might be able to retain control and regain the tarmac provided you are able to run parallel to the circuit for as long as it takes, then *ease* your way back on. Be *patient,* be smooth and don't do anything suddenly; if you are in too much of a hurry and try to wrestle the car back onto the tarmac you are almost certain to lose control.

Probably a last resort is to use the gravel trap. The one thing you are trying to avoid is contact with anything solid. If you conclude that a trip into the 'kitty litter' is inevitable it is preferable to drive straight in if possible, again keeping centrifugal force to a minimum. If you slew sideways into the gravel trap there is a chance the wheels will dig in and the car will roll. Even if you manage to avoid this you will have plenty of reason to curse after a trip into the gravel trap; the small stones have a habit of finding their way into every orifice, nook and cranny, and you will have hours of fun retrieving them all with a small brush, a vacuum cleaner and a screwdriver or whatever picking device comes to hand. Be sure to pick at least the worst of the stones out immediately afterwards, prior to doing the job properly, perhaps in the comfort of your own garage or workshop, as they can get jammed in the brake calipers and suspension components and do all sorts of damage if left. This is why the gravel traps are best avoided.

If you outbrake yourself, the greatest problem is that you have to assess your options very rapidly and make the right decisions, with no chance to practice, and usually no second chances. Is there an

Should you happen to run out of road and on to the grass, be patient, and ease the car back on to the circuit. If you are in too much of a hurry to regain the tarmac and steer or accelerate too sharply you are almost certain to lose control. Compared to the tarmac, the grass really is incredibly slippery. A famous F1 designer demonstrates.

If the gravel trap is the only thing between you and your car making a loud and expensive noise against the Armco, use it! Otherwise, the gravel traps are best avoided. Assuming you come safely to a halt, you will have to be towed out, which will probably cause the session to be stopped. You may be in for a bit of ribbing, but that is nothing to the hours of fun you will have picking stones out of every nook and cranny in your car's bodywork, chassis and suspension.

escape road? Can you spin harmlessly to a halt? Can you use the road width to make the braking area long enough to lose the excess speed? How much run-off area do you have to play with? Is the grass wet or dry? Is the gravel trap a safer bet? You may have to do some quick thinking and fancy steering to keep out of trouble. That is why I urge you to leave yourself some margin for error.

Taking the heat

Another reason to take it a little easier on the brakes is that it is much kinder to your car. Working the brakes really hard generates a ferocious amount of heat, which is the sworn enemy of all mechanical components. The heat generated by hard braking will rapidly wear out brake pads, may destroy the discs and can even melt the grease in wheel bearings *in extremis*. If

you habitually lock the brakes this will also kill the tyres, of course. You can greatly reduce the likelihood of mechanical carnage by warming the brakes thoroughly before using them hard and letting them cool down gradually afterwards.

Being smooth with the brakes, throttle and steering is a crucial element in fast driving, as I have said repeatedly, and smooth driving is about controlling or managing the weight transfer that takes place under acceleration, cornering and braking. The object of smooth braking, therefore, is to control the forward weight transfer as best we can. You have to accept that you can't affect *how much* weight is transferred, that being a function of wheelbase, centre of gravity height (both of which are fixed) and the g-force generated by braking which, although not fixed, we can assume to be a constant if the driver is

117

reasonably consistent in his braking effort. The driver, though, is the major influence in *how* the weight is transferred.

Smooth braking

If you get to your braking point and simply stand on the middle pedal you will get pronounced nosedive and in all probability will lock the brakes. Instead, when you start to brake you should apply gentle pedal pressure at first, building up pressure rapidly but smoothly so that you are applying firm pressure in the middle of the braking zone. You may end up pressing the brake pedal just as hard, but you have built up the load gradually and progressively rather than suddenly. Bear in mind, though, that when we talk about squeezing the brakes on, the difference between squeezing them on and slamming them on may be no more than a fraction of a second.

Just as important is to release the brakes smoothly. Some refer to this as 'feathering off' the brakes, which is as good a description as any. This means that the nose of the car comes back up to ride height smoothly and progressively rather than bouncing back up abruptly, perhaps even going past normal ride height as a result of the compressed suspension springs being suddenly released. The object is to have the car in a stable attitude when you turn into the corner. If you leave your braking to the last possible moment you are unlikely to be able to achieve this.

Clearly, judging how soon and how hard to brake for any given corner is a crucial aspect of the art of fast driving. The turn-in is perhaps the most important action on any corner as what you do at this point governs what happens right through the corner and all the way along any straight that follows. You have to turn in at the right place and at the right speed and move the steering wheel just the right amount (aiming to clip the corner apex), all the while remembering that your objective is to achieve the maximum possible acceleration out of the corner. In order to achieve the correct corner entry speed your braking distances and rate of deceleration must be judged to a nicety. You also need to

be in the right gear for maximum acceleration, of course.

Heel-and-toe

In the old days, before brakes were developed to their present peak of efficiency, braking distances were long and racing drivers needed to nurse their brakes if they were to last the entire race distance. They used engine braking – the drag created by compression – to assist the brakes in slowing the car, which meant that they changed down through each gear in turn. In order to change gear while braking, they evolved the technique of 'heeling-and-toeing', which allowed them to maintain pressure on the brake pedal while using the accelerator to assist gearchanges. In reality, rather than using heel and toe, most drivers used the side of their right foot to 'blip' the accelerator during downchanges (unless they were driving a Maserati 250F with a central accelerator, of course!), while continuing to press on the brake pedal with the ball of the foot. They also used the double-declutch method to synchronize engine revs with road speed for each gear, which speeded-up and smoothed-out their changes with the non-synchromesh gearboxes then in widespread use.

Nowadays brakes and gearboxes are so good that we don't need to double-declutch when changing down to save the gearbox, and we don't need to use engine braking to help the brakes. It is quite possible and perhaps even preferable, as some experts argue, to concentrate fully on braking hard and simply select the required gear at the end of the braking zone, just prior to turn-in. However, it is still desirable to blip the throttle on the downshift in order to match engine rpm and road speed for the chosen gear, to avoid 'snatching' the gearchange.

You should also strive to maintain even pressure on the brake pedal while blipping the throttle. The rate of deceleration should be as nearly constant as you can make it and there should be no appreciable change in the vehicle's attitude as a result of your gearchanges. Being smooth also helps you to develop a feel for what the car and, more importantly, the tyres are doing, whereas if you are rough and heavy-handed you will always be fighting the car. Moreover, you will probably feel that the car is fighting *you*.

The obvious corollary to this is that the faster you go the more difficult it becomes to be smooth. Even if you follow my advice and don't use your brakes to their fullest potential you will still be braking hard by road driving standards. You should *just* be able to complete your braking and gearchanging before you reach the turn-in point, so there is no discernible time lag between the end of the braking phase and the beginning of the cornering phase. If you find you are coasting the last few metres up to the turn-in point, you're not trying hard enough!

Trail braking

Some drivers take this to extremes and brake into the corners, perhaps right to the apex. This technique is known as trail braking. However, it is difficult for even the most adept drivers to achieve this with any worthwhile consistency, and it is only really feasible on the slower corners. So trail braking is probably best left to the experts until you have considerable experience, or perhaps until you have a chance to practice in a totally safe environment, such as an airfield.

As we have seen, there may be some overlap between the end of braking and the beginning of cornering, and there should certainly be considerable overlap between the end of cornering and the beginning of acceleration. These transitions should be made as quickly and seamlessly as possible so that the car, or more especially the tyres, should be working all the time. In other words, you should always be braking hard, cornering hard or accelerating hard, or some combination of these.

As far as practicable, you should try to blend and overlap the end of braking with the beginning of cornering, and the end of cornering with the beginning of acceleration. It is all about making the tyres give the maximum traction at all times, whether under acceleration, cornering or braking . . . though not all at the same time.

Under no circumstances should you be coasting, although I concede there may be one exception. Certain corners, which can be taken almost but not quite flat out, always present an interesting challenge. By their high-speed nature they tend to be somewhat daunting, and if you leave your braking to the last possible moment you tend to panic slightly and brake harder and slow down more than necessary. Far better, therefore, to take a calmer, more measured approach, braking early and gently, or even just lifting off the throttle early and not braking at all, to ensure the car is in a stable attitude before turning in. Effectively you will be coasting into the corner, but by doing so you may find it is possible to carry more speed into it than if you brake desperately late and try to turn in with the nose still buried into the tarmac!

Your corner entry speed should always be the highest that allows you to maintain maximum acceleration out. There is always a fine balance between too fast a corner entry and just fast enough. If we concentrate on getting a good exit from the bends there is a danger that we can become a bit lazy or complacent about the corner entry, so you should constantly analyse your approach to every corner and try to carry more speed into it. The moment your entry speed begins to compromise your ability to accelerate, and your exit speed, you know you have gone too far.

Don't try to go too fast too soon and remember that practice makes perfect; mastering these techniques will take time, patience and perseverance. If you concentrate and practice braking smoothly at all times you may often feel you could easily brake later and harder. You may well find, though (as I did!), that when you do you start making mistakes; locking up, missing turn-in points and apexes and generally making a complete hash of things. In trying to find the limit you realize that, almost by stealth and without being aware of it, you were already there! Rather than braking as late as possible, try thinking in terms of braking as *little* as possible. Remember what five-times World Champion Fangio said to a bemused rival when asked to explain his speed: "Less brakes; more accelerator"!

The dramatic effect of a grabbing front brake. Always remember that track days – unlike racing – are supposed to be non-competitive, so there is no incentive to use the brakes this hard. Also, you should strive to release the brakes as smoothly as you apply them.

15

DEALING WITH TRAFFIC

One of the trickiest aspects of driving on track for the first time is trying to keep out of the way of faster traffic while you are still learning the circuit and before you are fully up to speed. Most of the track day organizers operate the 'overtake on the left and move to the right when being overtaken' rule. This can cause problems for the novice when there are a lot of cars on circuit and you are travelling relatively slowly while still getting acclimatized to it, and possibly your car too. You will be concentrating intently and may well find the whole experience somewhat overwhelming. You may find that faster traffic forms a constant stream in your rear-view mirror, which forces you to keep to the right and prevents you from getting back onto the correct line to learn the circuit, which in turn prevents you from getting up to the speed which allows you to take your rightful place in the queue. It can be a vicious circle, one not easy to break.

However, there are a number of things you can do. The bigger the speed differential the greater the problem, so obviously it helps if you can go as fast as you feel comfortable with, or possibly even a bit faster. If you are too timid and creep around too slowly you can make it very difficult for yourself as you will be spending so much time looking in your mirrors and moving off line when you need to be concentrating on learning the circuit. On the other hand, you should never allow

yourself to be suckered into going too fast and getting in over your head simply from a well-meant desire not to impede others.

Remember you don't *have* to keep out of the way of faster traffic. As a matter of courtesy you should of course make every endeavour to do so, but not to the extent that it compromises your own ability to learn the circuit, or your enjoyment and safety. At many track days the organizers allow overtaking only on the straights, so on the basis that nobody is supposed to be overtaking on the corners anyway you are probably justified in ignoring what is behind you and concentrating instead on learning the lines through the corners. After all, it is in everybody's best interests for you to get up to speed as quickly as possible. Just take the normal line through the corner and move aside on the next straight, indicating if applicable to let faster traffic through.

If you find you are *really* slow relative to the other traffic and a queue quickly develops behind you, it may be advisable to slow right down on the next straight and allow the queue to clear, then get going again. When there is a gap in the traffic make the most of it by really concentrating on the next few corners or until such time as the next car looms in your mirrors. Obviously, if the organizers offer a novice session you should take advantage of it, along with any instruction that is on offer. If you are determined to learn and are at

Sometimes, even on a circuit, traffic is unavoidable when too many cars are allowed on track at one time. This is often a result of greedy or incompetent organizers selling too many places on a track day, either to cover costs or maximize profits. You may find that booking the cheapest track day is a false economy, and that paying a bit more results in better quality track time, a factor to bear in mind when booking.

least reasonably adept, and assuming your car is not too embarrassingly slow, pretty soon you will find that you are part of the normal traffic flow; not the quickest, perhaps, but not the slowest either. When you pass somebody for the first time you will have arrived!

Be decisive

When overtaking, be decisive, as dithering and indecision are usually the greatest cause of misunderstandings. However, it is impossible to lay down any hard-and-fast rules as to a great extent one must rely on the goodwill and good sense of all track day participants to make it as easy as possible for the novices. After all, we were all novices once. Every driver should remember that track days are strictly non-competitive, so if some novice wobbles into your path and spoils your 'hot' lap . . . so what? It ain't the final minute of qualifying for the Monaco Grand Prix! Remember that the onus is *always* on the overtaking driver to overtake safely.

Responsibility

Simple common sense tells us that the driver behind cannot help but see the car directly in front of him, whereas the driver ahead may not always see the vehicle behind. Regardless of the driver's experience, the mirrors do not offer a full field of vision, so the vehicle behind could well be in the driver's blind spot; but more likely is that the lead driver, especially if he is a track day novice, is concentrating far too intently on what is ahead to worry about what is behind . . . and rightly so! The safest approach for the overtaking driver is to *always* assume that the driver ahead has not seen him unless he can be absolutely sure otherwise. Some track day organizers suggest that the leading driver should indicate before moving off line to allow faster traffic through, not just to indicate his intention to move over but also to confirm to the following driver(s) that he has indeed seen them. That works well enough as long as everyone is prepared to co-operate, but the moment someone moves out of the way without indicating, or overtakes a driver who has not indicated, the system breaks down. It requires a lot of goodwill on everyone's part in order to operate successfully.

Sadly, the more participants there are at a track day the harder it becomes to achieve the requisite harmony and co-operation. For that reason it may be a good policy to choose your first track day where you know there will be few participants, or where the circuit rules allow only a few cars on track at a time. Some people seem to find it very difficult to accept being overtaken, or even the need to look in their rear-view mirrors from time to time, while others cannot tolerate being overtaken by a car they consider to be inferior (read 'less expensive'!) to their own. Sad . . . but unfortunately inflated egos can often get in the way of rational thought.

Frustration

It is a safe bet that all participants at a track day are enthusiasts, and it is reasonable to assume that most will have a keen interest in motorsport. It follows that some at least will be frustrated racing drivers, and despite the best efforts of the organizers to play this down, an element of competition tends to creep in on any track day. When your ability and confidence allows, it can be a good thing to set a personal goal to keep pace with a more experienced friend or colleague, say, or catch up with a car you have seen in the distance. A little competition is healthy, but you must be wary of getting into a real battle of egos where you become determined to pass someone who clearly is just as determined not to let you. There is nothing to be gained in this situation, and a lot to lose.

If you catch someone who is determined not to be overtaken, the best solution is not to bother; simply back off and allow him to get further ahead until you have a bit of clear track in front of you. You can then set yourself the challenge of catching up again, just to make the point! Alternatively you can let one or more other drivers overtake you and let them have the problem. You could also choose to have a quiet word in the pits afterwards, but in my experience it is unlikely to do much good. Conversely, if you have been caught by another competit . . . oops, I mean participant, you should allow him to overtake at the first opportunity, even if you think you or your car should be just as quick (the fact that he has caught up would suggest otherwise).

Indeed, cars of hugely dissimilar performance can often lap a circuit in very similar times. A good driver in a light car

Certain cars may achieve similar lap times in markedly different ways; Caterham is agile in the corners, but top speed and acceleration at higher speeds are limited by brick-like aerodynamics; Porsche is less nimble, but accelerates forever.

with good roadholding and acceleration but not much top speed (like a Caterham Seven or similar) can often go remarkably quickly, but the lap times are achieved with cornering speed and momentum. Cars that are more powerful but heavier can achieve the same lap times with slower cornering and higher straight-line speeds. Normally the more powerful car will slow the Seven-type machine in the corners, preventing its driver from maintaining precious momentum, which will make him (relatively) even slower on the straights. It is highly unlikely, however, that the Seven would ever impede the driver of the more powerful car, although different levels of driver skill and experience can obviously upset that equation.

Therefore if you find a Seven climbing all over you, you may need to ease off the throttle considerably on the straight to allow it by. Otherwise, if two cars achieve similar overall performance but in very different ways (*ie* fast on the straights, slow in the corners and *vice versa*), it can be very difficult to overtake in safety. If you were racing you would, of course, be perfectly entitled to make it as difficult as possible for anyone to overtake, and the driver behind would be entitled to take all reasonable risks to get by. But at a track day you're not racing, or at least you're not supposed to be. So if – through vanity, bloody-mindedness or whatever – you make it difficult for the following driver to overtake, unless he is mature enough to back off and find a clear stretch of track you more-or-less force him to take a risk in order to get by. If that should end in tears, whose fault would it be? I would suggest that the responsibility is at least equally shared; you're both bloody idiots!

Pass masters

Once you have completed a few track days you will doubtless have picked up speed, and instead of being preoccupied with keeping out of the way of faster traffic you can start to concentrate on how to overtake others. The essence of good clean overtaking is to gain momentum on someone and pass on the straight, although depending on the relative performance of

the two cars it may only be at the end of the straight – perhaps even in the braking zone – that you are able finally to make the pass. In order to gain sufficient momentum on the car ahead to pass it on the straight you need to negotiate the corner leading onto it at greater speed. Positioning and timing are crucial, the ideal being to emerge onto the straight just behind the other car, but travelling faster. If you catch up too soon you are forced to ease off the accelerator in order to avoid a collision and your momentum is lost. Conversely, if you arrive onto the straight too far behind you cannot get close enough to overtake.

Get it right, though, and depending on the power of the other car and how quickly it accelerates you can either follow it closely along the straight, taking advantage of the slipstream (much like following a lorry on the motorway) and pull out to overtake at the end; or if your speed is sufficient you may be able to breeze by immediately. Whatever speed advantage you can gain through the preceding corner is maintained all the way down the straight, and you would be *amazed* at how much extra power is needed to overcome that advantage. By timing your run to perfection (something that may take several attempts to achieve) it is often possible to overtake much more powerful cars in this way, so mastering this technique is extremely valuable. It is also much safer than trying to dive past under braking, or in the middle of a corner, even if this were allowed.

Remember that safety is always of paramount importance. If you have any doubt about being able to complete an overtaking manoeuvre safely you should err on the side of caution and abandon the attempt. There is absolutely nothing to be gained from making a marginal pass, if for no better reason than if things do go pear-shaped and you collide with another car there is simply no excuse. "I thought you'd seen me", or "I thought you were making room to let me through" just doesn't cut it. Everyone is at a track day to have fun, and staring ruefully at shattered glass, crumpled metal or shredded glassfibre is no fun in my book. Nor is a ride in an ambulance.

16

RIDING THE KERBS

At most circuits, the corners nowadays are lined by kerbs. In theory, the kerbs are supposed to define the circuit edges and drivers are supposed to stay within them; the kerbs are intended to give them a little safety margin in the event of running wide on the exit, or clipping an apex a little too closely, say. Inevitably, though, most racing drivers simply view kerbs as an extension of the circuit and they use them, especially on the exit, to widen the radius of the turn and hence go faster.

This gives the circuit owners and operators a thorny problem. If they make the kerbs low, smooth and gently contoured in order to fulfil their intended role as a safety feature, drivers inevitably will use them in order to go faster. But in doing so they obviously squander their safety margin, immediately rendering the kerbs redundant as a safety feature.

On the other hand, if they make the kerbs high, with sharp edges and perhaps a corrugated surface to discourage drivers from misusing them, they risk unsettling and possibly damaging cars that inadvertently stray onto them. Many of them are harsh enough to give the suspension quite a pounding. Front-wheel-drive cars certainly do not enjoy understeering into the kerbs with a lot of lock applied and power on as this plays havoc with the driveshafts. Cars routinely get thrown up onto two wheels after hitting a kerb awkwardly, and it is not unheard of

for saloons, with their inevitably higher centre of gravity, to capsize altogether. Low-slung single-seaters and purpose-built race cars can scrape their bellies on high kerbs, causing damage to their expensive aerodynamic floors, and because of their lack of ground clearance can even become grounded on the kerbs after a spin. Arguably, the high and aggressive kerbs designed to discourage drivers from using them as part of the circuit can create more of a hazard than no kerb at all. An amusing conundrum, for which there is no obvious solution.

Individual case
Unfortunately there is no apparent consensus and no commonality in the design of kerbs, all of which, therefore, should be approached with caution and every one treated as an individual case. You cannot generalize and simply say that at Donington Park, for example, it is safe to use the kerbs and at Oulton Park it is not. In order to assess whether it is safe, or indeed beneficial, to use the kerbs you need to drive over them – gently at first – and get a feel for how much they affect the balance of the car. If the car bounces or lurches unduly it is probably preferable to avoid that particular kerb, but if all is well, build up speed slowly until eventually you are confident to ride the kerbs at your usual pace. The behaviour of other cars and drivers on the circuit at the same time can

Kerbs are supposed to define the edges of a circuit and provide some margin for error. Race drivers however will habitually use kerbs to maximize corner radius. Make sure they do not unsettle the car unduly before using them in earnest.

provide another valuable clue: if others use the kerbs, it is reasonably safe to assume that you can do so, although you should always proceed with caution. With care and concentration you will soon develop an awareness of which kerbs you can safely use and which to avoid.

On a track day, where you are not perhaps chasing the last tenth of a second, I would advise against making too liberal use of the kerbs. Indeed, it can be considered quite an interesting challenge and good self-discipline to see how quickly you can go *without* using them.

Knock it off

If you *do* decide to use them you need to be aware of two things in particular. The first is brake pad knock-off, which I have already mentioned in *Brake Care and Cooling*. This can be caused by the corrugated kerbs found at some circuits and affects some cars worse than others (though some not at all), with small front-

wheel-drive saloons seeming to be particularly susceptible. What usually happens is that the corrugations set up a vibration in the front suspension, which causes the disc to shimmy within the brake caliper, which in turn pushes the pads back, forcing the caliper pistons back in their bores. Obviously this is exacerbated by any wear in the wheel bearings or other components of the front suspension.

The next time the brakes are applied, usually at the end of the following straight and hence at considerable speed, much or all of the pedal stroke is taken up just returning the pads into contact with the disc. In the worst case the pedal may go right to the floor, which feels disconcertingly like total brake failure and has much the same effect on a driver's peace of mind! Usually, a second stroke of the pedal is enough to restore normalcy, but if you are braking as late as possible you may not have time to lift off the brakes and apply them a second time, even assuming you have the presence of mind to do so.

The usual reaction of most drivers when confronted by an apparent brake failure is simply to press the brake pedal harder, which makes matters worse as all the braking effort is applied to the rear wheels. This can cause the rear brakes to lock up completely, which is guaranteed to get your attention! You really need to have your wits about you to remember to pump the pedal instead.

If you ever experience this you will soon learn to avoid such kerbs altogether, or if you find using one is unavoidable, to brush the brake pedal in order to take up the clearance and return the pads into contact with the discs just prior to applying the brakes again in earnest. This precautionary dab at the brakes just before the braking area soon becomes second nature.

Wet paint

The other thing to be extremely wary of is using the kerbs in the wet, as the highly durable high-gloss road marking paints used on them become notoriously slippery. Ask Nigel Mansell: he famously 'lost it' while leading a wet Monaco Grand Prix and clouted the barriers, putting him out of a race he looked likely to win. In this instance he strayed onto one of the painted road markings, not onto a kerb, but the principle is the same: the paints used in either case are *extremely* slippery and demand the utmost respect. Of course, driving a wet circuit demands even more discipline and circumspection, and that is the subject of *Handling the Wet*.

Remember, whereas some kerbs can be used to advantage, others will seriously upset the car and perhaps give you a busy time sorting out the consequences. This Mazda driver seems to have everything reasonably under control.

17

HANDLING THE WET

As motoring enthusiasts most of us will be familiar with the hazards of driving in the rain; poor visibility, reduced grip levels, standing water, and so on; let's face it, it's pretty unpleasant.

Racing in the rain is particularly stressful because of the impaired visibility when driving in close company with other vehicles. If you're to be competitive, though, you have no real alternative but to drive in close proximity to others, and if that means driving blind into a wall of spray, inches from a bunch of other drivers whose sanity is as questionable as your own, then so be it; the limited grip and traction may well be the least of your worries.

At the same time you may feel considerable pressure to put up a competitive showing, either because your team or sponsor expect you to produce results or simply because your own competitive nature causes you to put pressure on yourself. Whatever the cause, this will often lead you to go faster than you might prefer. When the conditions seem to be calling for prudence, patience and caution, your will to win is causing you to press the accelerator harder and earlier and leave your braking that fraction later. However, because of the reduced grip available the penalty for getting it wrong can be high. Miss your braking point by a few metres, brake marginally too hard or too late and you can all too easily lock up

and go off; prod the accelerator just a fraction too hard or too soon and you can be sliding ignominiously into the gravel traps or tyre walls. It's just *soooo* easy.

No worries
On a track day, however, you don't have to worry about all that. First, you can drive entirely at your own pace, however leisurely. If you are aware that you are driving markedly slower than anyone else (unlikely, as most will err on the side of caution), obviously it behoves you to keep a close eye on your mirrors and keep out of everyone's way as best you can. Under no circumstances, though, should you allow yourself to feel pressurized to go faster than you want to.

Another great advantage you have on a track day is that you should always be able to engineer a gap in the traffic so you can at least see where you're going. Even if this involves slowing right down to allow traffic to clear, or driving off line, it means you don't have to drive into great walls of spray.

Finally, you can choose not to go out at all if you prefer. Even here in the UK, during what we laughingly call the British summer, it is unlikely to rain hard all day, so if we are prepared to wait for half-an-hour or so conditions could well improve. Okay, the track may not dry out completely, but there is a good chance that conditions will be considerably better if you just wait for a short while. Of course, you

A wet track gives you an opportunity to practise your car control skills at relatively low speed, and without any pressure to be a hero.

may feel that this is losing you valuable track time.

Positive approach

Bearing all this in mind, if you find yourself at a wet track day, provided you are prepared to approach it in a positive way it can be an invaluable learning experience. And because there is no compulsion to go onto the circuit, you may find yourself on an all but deserted track with the opportunity to learn while everyone else waits for a break in the weather!

As we have seen, tyre grip levels will be considerably reduced in wet conditions, for two reasons. First, the coefficient of friction is reduced because the water on the road surface and on the tyre acts as a lubricant. Second, and less obviously perhaps, the tyres may be cooled by the wet road surface

so they don't attain their optimum temperature. However, this needn't cause any undue problems provided you proceed with caution and treat the conditions with respect. If the track is smooth and well drained, so it doesn't attract standing water, driving in the wet can even be fun, especially if you can go around at your own pace with no pressure to go fast. Often you can get the feel of a car sliding around at much reduced pace, and it gives you the opportunity to muck about and experiment – using different lines, deliberately inducing slides and so on – if your confidence allows.

In the wet, because of the lack of grip, the need for smoothness is even greater to avoid disturbing the tyres' even more tenuous hold on the tarmac. A useful trick is to use a gear higher than you would in the dry, which makes it less likely you will inadvertently spin the wheels with an injudicious prod of the throttle. A smooth engine with ample torque will prove much easier to drive than a peaky, 'revvy' one. Incidentally, have you ever noticed how your engine seems to go better when it is wet? Well, it does. Your engine will revel in the cool damp oxygen-rich air it is getting on a rainy day and will go like a rocket. If you are even slightly cautious it shouldn't cause you any problems, but it is something to bear in mind when you are approaching your braking point at the end of a long straight, or accelerating out of a slow corner.

Adjustments

It may also be possible to make some minor adjustments to the car to help you cope with the more slippery conditions. Because of the reduced grip available from the tyres, weight transfer will be somewhat reduced. You may find, for example, that you don't get as much forward weight transfer under braking so you will tend to lock the front brakes prematurely if the bias is optimized for dry conditions. If your vehicle has adjustable brake bias, transferring some braking effort to the rear will help to maintain optimum brake balance. Don't forget to return the bias as the track dries, though!

Similarly, because lateral weight transfer in cornering is reduced, you may want to consider softening the dampers and perhaps softening or even disconnecting one or both anti-roll bars. This general 'softening' of the car should allow you to get more feel for the tyres and the level of grip available. Of course, this presupposes that these adjustments are easy and practicable to achieve; don't feel that you *have* to change suspension settings or brake bias in order to drive safely in the wet. You should always drive to the conditions, bearing in mind your own ability and confidence and the performance capabilities of your car. If you are tempted to make changes to the car, always be sure to feel them out during the first few laps out of the pits.

It may also be beneficial to adjust your lines to try to find some grippier tarmac by seeking out less used parts of the track.

Many circuits, especially when they have not been resurfaced for a long while, develop a 'groove' on the optimum racing line where the tarmac is polished smooth by the passage of innumerable tyres. This often takes on a real sheen when wet. If it looks slippery it usually is! You may find considerably more grip and traction are available by straying from the optimum line onto the less well-used bits of tarmac where the stones are not polished smooth. Indeed, some circuits – Brands Hatch is one – are known to have a 'wet' line which is completely at odds with the conventional racing line. Again, provided you act with prudence and caution you should be able to experiment to find the optimum wet line for yourself.

Aquaplaning

As I have said, I would always encourage you to treat a wet circuit as a challenge and a positive learning experience. There is, however, one wet-weather driving hazard that I would view with a respect approaching fear: aquaplaning! Also sometimes referred to as hydroplaning, this occurs when a tyre passes through standing water at such a speed that the tread channels are unable to disperse the surface water quickly enough. A wedge of water builds up in front of the tyre, lifting the tread clear of the road surface. This is extremely dangerous because no amount of driving skill will help you when your tyres are not in contact with the track.

Anyone who has ever experienced this phenomenon will know the true meaning of fear as there is absolutely *nothing* you can do to maintain control. The only thing you can do is ease off the accelerator as gently as possible, resist any temptation to brake, and keep the steering wheel as straight as you can – don't even *breathe* – and hope. You might get away with it, but don't kid yourself that anything you may have done had anything to do with it; the only thing that saved you was dumb luck!

The factors that induce aquaplaning, apart from the depth of the standing water, are speed, tread depth and tyre width. Assuming you can't suddenly and miraculously increase your tread depth or reduce your tyre width, the only thing you can do to prevent aquaplaning is slow down! Therefore, if there is standing water on the circuit I strongly advise you to simply park the car until it disperses. There is nothing to be gained from splashing around at much reduced pace, and potentially much to be lost if you hit a large puddle just fractionally too fast. You will not *believe* how suddenly and irretrievably control can be lost.

Aside from that, though, a wet track is something to be welcomed rather than feared. It is all part of the total track day driving experience in which you can enjoy a wonderful variety of straights and curves on tarmac shaped and prepared for performance, safety and entertainment, and without so much as a speed camera, radar gun or sleeping policeman in sight. No wonder track days have become so popular!

Wet-track practice can be both educational and enjoyable, but stay in the pits when it is pouring because of the risk of aquaplaning, when even the most accomplished driver can do little more than trust to luck.

18

FINDING THE LIMIT

It should be obvious by now that driving fast . . . *really* fast, on a race circuit is an immensely demanding and difficult activity. You will often hear racing drivers talking about being 'on the limit', so it may be logical to assume that they are *always* on the limit. But they're not. Even the world's leading Formula One drivers admit they cannot drive at qualifying pace for an entire race distance; it requires too much effort and concentration, takes too much out of the car and it's too risky. Even in qualifying, when all they have to do is *one lap* as fast as possible, they don't necessarily get the best out of the car or the tyres. They may make tiny mistakes – probably indiscernible outside the cockpit – that take them just over the limit, or they may stay just under the limit in order to avoid making those mistakes. Afterwards they curse themselves for taking too many risks . . . or too few!

Big egos
Racing drivers are intrinsically an egotistical lot, and some may resent the implication that they are not flat-out all the time, but the more intelligent and thoughtful drivers accept that there is *always* something left. Sir Stirling Moss often alluded to this, maintaining that he had never achieved the perfect lap, despite being the best of his generation. More recently Ayrton Senna said that whenever he achieved a lap on what he thought was

the limit, all it did was cause him to redefine the limit. And this was the guy who scored 65 pole positions in a glittering Formula One career, a record that may never be surpassed. Certainly no one was faster over a single lap, no one more committed. The point is that 'the limit' is elusive, even for the very best.

Mistakes
There are a number of reasons why we cannot drive on the limit at all times. First is that no matter how skilled or accomplished we may become, we will inevitably make those little mistakes. We may brake a metre or two too late, turn in a fraction too early or too late, turn the wheel a touch too much or too little, stray from the perfect line by just a few inches, apply a bit too much throttle too soon, and so on.

Obviously the faster you go the more likely you are to make a mistake because the less time you have to process inputs; and by the same token, of course, the more quickly you need to react to them. In driving, as when performing any skilled task, it is when we are forced to hurry that we are most likely to make mistakes. Astronauts and test pilots are tested and specifically selected for their ability to perform complex tasks under pressure. This pressure usually comes in the form of a requirement for speed; but other forms of pressure may include extreme heat, noise, high g-loadings, etc. Sound familiar? Yes, racing drivers habitually cope with all of those things . . . *at the same time*. Not only that, but for trainee astronauts, test pilots and the like, this pressure is usually simulated, and occurs in a test environment (although there may be occasional alarming exceptions!). But for racing drivers, the pressure is real; their lives literally may depend on their making the right moves.

The obvious corollary to this is that the faster you go the more serious the consequences of any mistake. When you are driving well below the limit – while waving to the crowd on the slow-down lap, for example! – you can stray from the ideal line with relative impunity. However, when you are cornering very near the limit the line is crucial. Make a mistake at the turn-in point, for example, and you can all too easily drop a couple of wheels off the road on the exit, perhaps 200 metres further on. At the very least, this will cause you to back off the throttle while you regain the circuit and, possibly, your composure too! The loss of precious momentum and the lack of acceleration will be felt all the way along the next straight, so any such minor excursion will inevitably result in a loss of time. At worst it could cause you to lose control.

As I have already demonstrated, your cornering speed is critical to within a fraction of a mile per hour and your line is critical to within a few inches; you are working to very fine margins. The point is that when you are at the limit, going only very slightly beyond it (entering a corner half-a-mile per hour too fast, say, or straying 6 inches off the road on the exit) can lead to disaster, whereas if you are very slightly under the limit you will usually get away with it . . . which is why they call it a margin for error I suppose.

Pragmatism

Which brings me to the second major reason we cannot be on the limit all the time, and it is a purely pragmatic one. When we make mistakes as described we stand to lose more than we might otherwise gain. In other words we may seek to gain a tenth of a second by tackling a corner just that fraction faster, but if we get it wrong it is all too easy to lose 2 or 3 seconds and (ignoring the possibility that we might even crash!) perhaps much more, with a spin or a trip up the escape road. It can be likened to

Although Ayrton Senna was the fastest driver of his generation, and possibly the fastest ever, even he found The Limit elusive. At Monaco in 1988, he found that the nearer he got to the limit the further away it became.

a form of gambling where the potential gains are very small and the potential losses very large; imagine taking a bet where you might win a quid if you're right but lose £100 if you're wrong. Not many people would be tempted by those odds! In a race, the loss of even 5 seconds with a minor mistake can be extremely difficult, perhaps impossible, to recover. For that reason even the very best drivers leave themselves some margin for error, albeit a tiny one.

The wet patch

Another reason it is not possible to drive at the absolute limit of adhesion at all times is that in any given corner you can only drive to the *minimum* grip available simply because you cannot make instantaneous changes to your line and speed to take account of minor variations in grip. To make an extreme and slightly silly example, imagine a long fast corner that is perfectly dry, bar an extremely slippery patch caused by a large puddle right on the apex. If you were to attempt the corner at the usual 'dry' pace, relying on the grip you have in the dry, you would almost certainly have a nasty surprise when you hit the wet patch. A wild slide would be a virtual certainty. If you were to drive the dry line as well, that slide would put you – assuming you didn't simply lose control – onto a wider line that would be virtually guaranteed to take you off the road edge at the exit.

Conversely, there is no need to drive the entire corner as though it were wet. What you would do in fact is slow down somewhat and modify your line to allow you to cross the wet portion of track with the front wheels straightened, or nearly so. In reality the situation is seldom so clear cut; you will find there are ordinarily only very minor variations in grip, caused by surface changes, elevation changes (the car going 'light' over a crest is a particular favourite), bumps in the road or perhaps some quirk in the vehicle's handling. In broad terms, therefore, the speed you can take the corner is dictated by the grip you have on the most slippery bit, although you may be able to modify your line somewhat to minimize the effect. In fact you will probably find you do this instinctively anyway, so there is no need to think too much about it.

Facing your fears

Possibly the final factor that prevents you from finding the limit is fear; fear of the unknown, of crashing, hurting yourself, damaging your car, looking foolish or upsetting your wife/girlfriend/bank manager (perhaps all three!). However brave we may try to be or think we are, at some subliminal level we perceive danger in speed, and our innate caution and sense of self-preservation takes over and keeps us from going right to the edge for fear of straying inadvertently over it. It is a built-in natural defence mechanism designed to prevent us from harming ourselves.

From all that you have read so far it should be apparent that fast driving is all about getting as near to the edge as you can without actually going over it. Some wag once likened it to seeing how far you can lean out of an upper-storey window without actually falling out, and that's not a bad summation. Fear of falling is what prevents us from leaning out that little bit further. In the end it is all about pushing yourself, and that is one of the great attractions of fast driving. It is a *challenge*, and the challenge derives from confronting your fears and perhaps overcoming them.

Challenge

That challenge exists for racing drivers (and here we can put track day drivers in the same category) as it does for mountaineers, aerobatic pilots, extreme skiers and assorted other daredevils who, like us, are addicted to adrenaline. Our bodies naturally produce this performance-enhancing drug in response to fear, and this is what gives us *the buzz*.

These adventure sports all have one thing in common, and that is the *frisson* of danger, and that's what makes them so irresistibly attractive to the adventurous spirit. In taking on this challenge, though, don't forget that you're meant to be enjoying yourself. Because driving fast demands a high level of concentration, it is easy to become altogether too serious and intense (for evidence of this, just check any

Formula One paddock!), especially if you place unrealistic expectations on yourself. By all means push yourself to do better, but remember you should be pushing yourself to your own personal limits, not someone else's.

You might well find that you don't enjoy pushing your car or yourself right to the limit; that doing so is just too difficult, stressful and . . . let's face it, too damned scary. You may also find that *your* fast is not as fast as somebody else's and that in fact it is not that fast after all . . . a realization that comes to most of us sooner or later. So what? Above all, don't allow yourself to be suckered into going beyond your abilities by bravado and peer pressure (mostly fuelled by paddock bullshit!) or by putting unrealistic expectations on

yourself. Remember that *nobody* can drive consistently to the car's limits, and therefore you should always drive to *your own* limits.

If every time you attend a track day you can push back your threshold of fear little by little and at the same time develop your skills, a great deal of enjoyment and satisfaction will be yours. Bear in mind that the best drivers in the world cannot achieve the perfect lap, so strive to do so by all means, but don't expect to 'crack it' any time soon. Perhaps that's just as well because if ever we *did* drive a perfect lap there would be no point in carrying on, would there? The search for the perfect lap – which could be likened to the Holy Grail of track day drivers – gives us a reason to continue, and long may it do so.

A posed picture, admittedly, but it delivers an important message to track day drivers: perhaps you are the fortunate owner of a performance car, but if not, however modest your set of wheels, provided your car is mechanically sound and well maintained, take it on to the track and enjoy a quality of driving which has long been banned on public roads. You'll enjoy every minute of it, I promise you.

19

TO SUMMARIZE

I hope you have read the previous 18 chapters and found things of value in each of them. If so, I am sure you will be better equipped to gain the maximum enjoyment and value for money out of your track day exploits.

Of all the adrenaline sports available to you, driving fast on track days is perhaps the most accessible. All you need is a roadworthy car (okay, it helps if it is at least reasonably fast, but this is by no means essential), some safety equipment, and a positive approach to learning. It's challenging, exciting, stimulating, exhilarating . . . with the additional benefit that all that you learn on the race track will benefit your road driving skills.

That is not to suggest that they are similar: quite the opposite in fact. On the road you cannot negotiate the same corner every few minutes in order to get your braking point, turn-in point, entry speed and line *exactly* right. Conversely, on the circuit you don't have to worry about staying on the right side of the road, traffic coming the other way, parked cars, speed limits, traffic lights and other hazards of the open road. For that reason the two disciplines are totally different. Whereas on a circuit you can go as fast as the vehicle and your own skill (and nerve!) allows, on the road you are usually constrained by speed limits, respect for other road users and the requirement to stay on the correct side of the road; but above all because as a

responsible road user you should always leave a reasonable margin of safety to allow for the unexpected. Dare I suggest that only by driving on a circuit can you begin to appreciate the distinction, despite whatever your ego may tell you.

Because the driving environment is so very different, the demands you make from a car are also different. Indeed, the car you always thought was so fast and responsive on the road may prove to be a very different animal on the circuit; the engine may seem sluggish, the handling soggy and the brakes poor, so in order to enjoy your circuit time more you may consider making some improvements. You should be aware though that every aspect of a vehicle's design is a compromise and that anything you do to improve your car for circuit use may have a detrimental effect on the road. Therefore you must always assess whether the pros outweigh the cons.

Safety should be your first priority, but bear in mind that *absolute* safety is not achievable. Driving fast is essentially a hazardous activity and therefore the best you can achieve, and thus what you should strive for, is an *acceptable* level of safety. You should be aware that even the modifications you make in the cause of safety may have a downside in rendering the car less practicable for road use, or even to have a detrimental effect on safety on the road. The best and most obvious example of this is the full rollcage. A full cage

Only you can decide whether the risks you take on a track day can justify the investment in safety equipment. If you have done so, however, it makes sense to wear your gear every time you venture on to the circuit.

undoubtedly enhances the strength, rigidity and structural integrity of a passenger car habitacle (as the FIA is wont to call the bit where the people sit) and therefore will enhance safety in the event of a serious shunt on track. However, many of the tubes that constitute the cage unavoidably run perilously close to the inhabitants' heads. They are intended for use with helmets, so this is seldom any problem on the circuit, but in the unfortunate event of an accident on the road the cage may be just as likely to cause injury as prevent it. I have tried to point out most of the drawbacks of fitting competition equipment to your road car, but only you can decide whether the fitting of competition seats, full-harness seat belts, plumbed-in fire extinguisher and so on are worth the hassle and expense, bearing in mind the inherent compromises.

In order to ensure safety and reliability you should establish an appropriate maintenance schedule, again having regard to the greatly accelerated wear and tear inherent in circuit use. You may need to inspect and replace parts, in particular high-wear items like brake pads and tyres, on a much more frequent and regular basis. Keeping a careful log of your mileage will help you keep tabs on the vehicle's maintenance requirements, especially if you use it for mixed road and track driving. Despite the oil manufacturers' claims, I would also recommend changing oil much more frequently than the schedule noted in your vehicle manufacturer's service book.

You should always aim to arrive at the circuit for a track day in good time and with the car ready for action. This may seem obvious, but it is amazing how often you see people wasting valuable track time performing routine maintenance tasks that should really have been done in the workshop beforehand, especially if they are safety-related. Okay, finding that you have to change a set of spark plugs at the circuit is not a total disaster, but discovering that you really should have installed a new set of brake pads might be! Remember that prevention is better than cure.

Only when you are satisfied that your

If you have paid good money to attend a track day, it is important to arrive with the car ready to run, and not to waste valuable track time in performing routine maintenance chores.

car is safe and reliable should you consider making modifications to enhance performance. There are very few performance-enhancing modifications you can make that will not compromise the vehicle in some way, especially if you mean to use it on the road, so the effect of everything you do must be very carefully considered. You need to balance the likely benefit of every mod with the likely drawbacks, giving adequate consideration to how frequently you will do track days, and to what extent and for what purposes you need to use the vehicle on the road. If you only ever drive the vehicle to and from track days or for fun, then you can afford to compromise much more than if you wish to use it for a family touring holiday, for example.

Your priorities should be to improve braking, roadholding and handling before searching for any power increase. Improving the suspension and brakes will enable you to further develop your driving skills, which will in turn allow you to better exploit the power you have got, whereas

more power will likely prove an embarrassment. And although you should – in theory! – not be paying much attention to lap times, it is a virtual certainty that better roadholding will prove more beneficial to lap times than more engine power.

Indeed, it is arguable whether you should undertake any modifications to improve performance until such time as your driving skill allows you to exploit your chosen track day vehicle to the full. In fact you can attend a track day with nothing more than a bog-standard, albeit sound and well-maintained road car, and a good-quality crash helmet. If you have even a whiff of petrol in your veins, I can virtually guarantee you will have a ball. What you learn from a day of high-speed driving on a race circuit will make you a smoother, faster and safer driver. You will have a better idea of the skills required in true high-speed driving. You may develop an awareness of how quickly and easily things can go wrong at speed, and the possible consequences. Even more beneficial, perhaps, regular attendance at track days may enable you to control your need for speed, so you are no longer tempted to risk life, limb and licence with excessive speed on the open road.

As we have seen, conducting a high-performance car around a race circuit at high speed is a highly skilled activity, and I hope that I may have shed some light on an inordinately complex subject. Perhaps the single most important principle to remember from our discussion on vehicle dynamics is the need to obtain maximum acceleration at all times. Even though motor vehicles have improved enormously, the time-honoured slow in − fast out principle still applies.

Of course, this theoretical wisdom is all very well, but you can hardly drive around a racing circuit at high speed with this book open and spread across your knees, can you? We may theorize all we wish about slip angles, and weight transfer, and lines, and acceleration, and the right corner radius . . . *ad infinitum*. But there is absolutely no substitute for simply getting out there and doing it. However much you may study the subject, read up on it, or watch instructional videos, driving must be hands-on; there is simply no substitute for experience.

It is commonly assumed that racing drivers need fast reactions, but it is more important to have the right reactions than the quickest reactions, and for that you need to be able to anticipate what the car will do. Anticipation, therefore, is much preferable to reaction. But unfortunately, anticipation can only be gained through experience, so you know what to expect; sadly, there is no short cut or totally safe means to acquire that experience. At least learning in the relative safety of a closed race track is preferable to doing so on the open road. I sincerely hope that gaining the necessary experience doesn't exact too high a cost. The most important thing is to take your time; you cannot expect to be on the pace immediately.

Driving a car in a sporting manner, whether in competition or just for fun as in a track day, is different to most other sports and games in that mistakes can be costly. When you are learning to play tennis, for example, if you hit a poor shot you can simply retrieve the ball and try again. If you miss-hit a golf shot you can simply replace the divot and have another whack. When learning to play the piano, if you hit a bum note you can always stop and 'take it from the top'. But when you are learning to drive a car up to the limit of its performance, making a mistake can cause serious damage and financial loss, not forgetting possible human injury or worse.

It therefore behoves you to always consider the art of fast driving seriously. Have fun, of course, but never forget that a car in less than adequate hands can be a dangerous toy. Despite those words of warning, I hope I may have encouraged you to have a go. I promise you, you'll enjoy every minute of it.

APPENDIX

Useful addresses and contact numbers

(Inclusion in the following listing does not necessarily imply endorsement by the author, nor does omission from it infer the contrary. The number of track day venues and organizers is increasing constantly and readers are recommended to consult current motorsport journals for up-to-date information on the latest developments and facilities.)

TRACK DAY ORGANIZERS

The Gold Track Driving Club
Little Preston House
Little Preston
Northamptonshire
NN11 3TF
Tel: 01327 361361
www.gtdc@cix.co.uk

Trackstar Circuit Days Ltd
29 Wheelers Road
Midsomer Norton
Bath
BA3 2BX

Wheeltorque Ltd
29 Station Road West
Trimdon Station
County Durham
TS29 6BP
www.info@wheeltorque.net

On-Track Experience
11 The Spinnaker
South Woodham Ferrers
Essex
CM3 5GL
www.h@ontrackexperience.co.uk

Driving Development
PO Box 711
Maidenhead
Berkshire
SL6 1XT
www.drivingdevelopment.co.uk

Limelight Exhibitions Ltd
1 Howard Road
Reigate
Surrey
RH2 7JE
www.limelight-exhibitions.co.uk

Lloyd's Motor Club
Lloyds of London
1 Lime Street
London
EC3M 7HL
www.lloydsmotorclub.com

Castle Combe
www.emma@castlecombecircuit.co.uk

RMA
Tel: 01628 779000
www.rma-limited.co.uk

Trackfun
www.trackfun.co.uk

BookaTrack
www.bookatrack.com

Easytrack
Tel: 01785 661418
www.easytrack.co.uk

Motorsport Events Ltd
www.motorsport-events.co.uk

Fastrack
www.fastrackracing.com

Track Sense
www.tracksense.co.uk

A comprehensive Track Day Diary is printed in Circuit News, a magazine available on subscription only from the publishers:
What's On Motorsport Ltd
Newbarn Court
Ditchley Park
Chipping Norton
Oxfordshire
OX7 4EX.

Also check out
www.circuitdriver.com.

CIRCUITS – UK

Anglesey
c/o Track Sense
Cricketers Lane
Windlesham
Surrey
GU20 6HA
Tel: 01276 473616
www.tracksense.co.uk

Bedford Autodrome
Thurleigh Airfield Business
Park
Bedfordshire
MK44 2YP
Tel: 01403 733999
Fax: 01403 733222

Brands Hatch
Fawkham
Dartford
Kent
DA3 8NG
Tel: 01474 872331
Fax: 01474 874766

Cadwell Park
The Venue Office
Cadwell Park
Louth
Lincolnshire
LN11 9SE
Tel: 01507 343248
Fax: 01507 343519

Castle Combe
Chippenham
Wiltshire
SN14 7EY
Tel: 01249 782417
Fax: 01249 782392

Croft
Croft on Tees
North Yorkshire
DL2 2PN
Tel: 01325 721815
Fax: 01325 721819

Donington Park
Castle Donington
Derbyshire
DE74 2RP
Tel: 01332 810048
Fax: 01332 850422

Goodwood
Chichester
West Sussex
PO18 0PH
Tel: 01243 755060
Fax: 01243 755065

Knockhill
By Dunfermline
Fife
KY12 9TF
Tel: 01383 723337
Fax: 01383 620167

Llandow
Cowbridge
Vale of Glamorgan
CG71 7PB
Tel: 01446 796460
www.enquiries@llandow.com

Mallory Park
Kirkby Mallory
Leicestershire
LE9 7QE
Tel: 01455 842931
Fax: 01455 848289

Oulton Park
Little Budworth
Tarporley
Cheshire
CW6 9BW
Tel: 01829 760301
Fax: 01829 760378

Pembrey
BARC (Pembrey) Ltd
Llanelli
Carmarthenshire
SA16 0HZ
Tel : 01554 891042
Fax : 01554 891387

Rockingham
PO Box 500
Corby
Northamptonshire
NN17 5RR
Tel: 0870 0134044
Fax: 01536 500555

Silverstone
Silverstone Circuit
Nr Towcester
Northamptonshire
NN12 8TN
Tel:01327 857271
Fax: 01327 857188

Snetterton
Nr Attleborough
Norwich
Norfolk
NR16 2JU
Tel: 01953 887303
Fax: 01953 888220

Thruxton
BARC
Thruxton Circuit
Andover
Hampshire
SP11 8PN
Tel: 01264 882200
Fax: 01264 882233

CIRCUITS – EEC

A1-Ring
A-8724 Spielberg
Austria
Tel: +43 3577 753
Fax: +43 3577 753 107

Salzburgring
Molkhofgasse 3
A-5020 Salzburg
Austria
Tel: +43 662 84 87 34
Fax: +43 662 84 87 344

Spa-Francorchamps
Route de Circuit 55
4970 Francorchamps
Belgium
Tel: +32 8727 55258
Fax: +32 8727 5296

Zolder
Controltoren
Terlamen 30
3550 Heusden
Zolder
Belgium
Tel: +32 87 774040
Fax: +32 87 774740

Albi
Route de Toulouse
81990 Le Sequestre
Albi
France
Tel: +33 5 6343 2300
Fax: +33 5 6343 2301

Croix-en-Ternois
Route Nationale 39
Croix-en-Ternois
France
Tel: +33 3 2103 3013
Fax: +33 3 2103 2720

Le Mans
AC de l'Ouest
Circuit des 24 Heures
72019 Le Mans
Cedex 2
France
Tel: +33 2 4340 2424
Fax: +33 2 4340 2425

Magny-Cours
Circuit de Nevers
58470 Magny-Cours
France
Tel: +33 3 8621 8000
Fax: +33 3 8621 8080

Montlhery
UTAC
Autodrome de Linas Montlhery
91310 Montlhery
France
Tel: +33 1 6980 1700
Fax: +33 1 6980 1704

Nogaro
Circuit Paul Armagnac
BP24
32110 Nogaro
France
Tel: +33 5 6209 0249
Fax: +33 5 6269 0544

Pau
c/o ASAC Basco Bearnais
1 Boulevard Aragon
64000 Pau
France
Tel: +33 5 5927 3189
Fax: +33 5 5927 6169

Paul Ricard
Route Nationale 8
83330 Le Beausset
France
Tel: +33 4 9490 7960
Fax: +33 4 9490 7275

Hockenheim
D-68766 Hockenheim
Motodrom Germany
Tel: +49 6205 9500
Fax: +49 6205 950299

Lausitz
Eurospeedway
Lausitzallee 1
01998 Klettwitz
Germany
Tel: +49 35 754 31110
Fax: +49 35 754 31111

Norisring
Motor Sport Club Nurnberg im ADAC
Aussere Sulzbacherstrasse 98
94091 Nurnberg
Germany
Tel: +49 911 597051
Fax: +49 911 597052

Nurburgring
53520 Nurburg/Eifel
Germany
Tel: +49 2691 3020
Fax: +49 2691 302155

Oschersleben
Motopark Allee 20-22
39387 Oschersleben
Germany
Tel: +49 3949 9200
Fax: +49 3949 920660

Sachsenring
Am Sachsenring
D-09353 Oberlungwitz
Germany
Tel: +49 3723 65330
Fax: +49 3723 653355

Hungaroring
Pf 10 Office
Hungaroring Sport Rt
2146 Mogyorod
Hungary
Tel: +36 28 444 444
Fax: +36 28 441 860

Mondello Park
Donore
Naas
County Kildare
Ireland
Tel: +353 45 860200
Fax: +353 45 860195

Imola
Circuit Enzo & Dino Ferrari
Sagis SpA
Via F Rosselli 2
40026 Imola (BO)
Italy
Tel: +39 0542 31444
Fax: +39 0542 30420

Misano
Autodromo Santamonica
Via del Carro 27A
I-47843 Misano
Adriatico (RN)
Italy
Tel: +39 0541 618511
Fax: +39 0541 615463

Monza
20052 Monza Parco (MI)
Italy
Tel: +39 039 24 821
Fax: +39 039 32 0324

Vallelunga
ACI Sport
Via Cassia
Bivio km34.5
00063 Campagnano di Roma
Italy
Tel: +39 069 015 501
Fax: +39 069 042 197

Zandvoort
PO Box 132
2040 AC Zandvoort
Netherlands
Tel: +31 23 574 0740
Fax: +31 23 574 0741

Estoril
Circuito do Estoril
Estrada Nacional 9
Km6 Apartado 49
2646-901 Alcabideche
Portugal
Tel: +35 21 460 9500
Fax: +35 21 460 9595

Enna
Autodromo Pergusa
Enna
Sicily
Tel: +39 25660/641069
Fax: +39 25825/541344

Barcelona
Circuit de Catalunya
Mas la Moreneta
Apartado de Correos 27
08160 Montmelo (Barcelona)
Spain
Tel: +34 93 571 9700
Fax: +34 93 572 3061

Jarama
RACE
Ctra N1 km27, 800
28700 San Sebastian de Los
Reyes (Madrid)
Spain
Tel: +34 1657 0785
Fax: +34 1652 2744

Jerez
Ctra de Arcos
km10, Apdo de Correos 1709
Jerez de la Frontera (Cadiz)
Spain
Tel: +34 956 151107
Fax: +34 956 151105

Valencia
Aptdo Correos 101
46380 Cheste
Valencia
Spain
Tel: +34 96 351 4977
Fax: +34 96 351 4975

Anderstorp
Scandinavian Raceway
Box 180
S-33424 Anderstorp
Sweden
Tel: +46 371 16170
Fax: +46 371 16177

Karlskoga
Gellerasen
Box 296
S-69125 Karlskoga
Sweden
Tel: +46 586 15010
Fax: +46 586 15049

CIRCUITS – USA & Canada

Charlotte
5555 Concord Parkway South
Harrisburg
North Carolina 28075
USA
Tel: +1 704 455 3200
Fax: +1 704 455 3237

Chicago
3301 South Laramie Avenue
Cicero
Illinois 60804
USA
Tel: +1 773 242 2277
Fax: +1 773 242 2278

Daytona
1801 West International
Speedway Boulevard
Daytona Beach
Florida 32114-1243
USA
Tel: +1 909 472 700
Fax: +1 909 476 791

Elkhart Lake
Road America Inc
Elkhart Lake
Wisconsin 53020
USA
Tel: +1 920 892 4576
Fax: +1 920 892 4550

Homestead
1 Speedway Boulevard
Homestead
Florida 33035-1501
USA
Tel: +1 305 230 5000
Fax: +1 305 230 5223

Indianapolis
4790 West 16th Street
Indianapolis
Indiana 46222
USA
Tel: +1 317 484 6780
Fax: +1 317 484 6482

Laguna Seca
1021 Monterey
Salinas Highway
Salinas
California 93908
USA
Tel: +1 831 648 5111
Fax: +1 831 373 0533

Mid-Ohio
PO Box 3108
Steam Corners Road
Lexington
Ohio 44904
USA
Tel: +1 419 884 4000
Fax: +1 419 884 0042

Portland
PO Box 3024
Portland
Oregon 97208
USA
Tel: +1 503 232 3000
Fax: +1 503 232 2336

Sebring
113 Midway Drive
Sebring
Florida 33870
USA
Tel: +1 863 655 1442
Fax: +1 863 655 1777

Mosport
Panoz Motor Sports
3233 Concession Road No 10
Bowmanville
Ontario L1C 3K6
Canada
Tel: +1 905 983 9141
Fax: +1 905 983 5195

Trois-Rivieres
Terrain de l'Exposition
883 Boulevard des Forges
Bureau 201
Trois-Rivieres
Quebec
Canada
Tel : +1 819 373 9912
Fax : +1 819 373 9678

ACKNOWLEDGEMENTS

For their valued assistance in making this publication possible, the author thanks: Demon Tweeks, purveyors of the very best in racewear and motorsport paraphernalia to the cognoscenti; RMA, for making us welcome to take photographs at one of their excellent track days; John Colley, for his excellent images from that day; and Jeff Bloxham, for additional photography. And thanks to my beautiful wife Carol...